THE GUILT TRIP

GETTING OFF A
DEAD-END STREET

THE GUILT TRIP

GETTING OFF A DEAD-END STREET

Gary E. Parker

McCracken Press
New York

McCracken Press™
An imprint of Multi Media Communicators, Inc.
575 Madison Avenue, Suite 1006
New York, NY 10022

The events described in this book are true. In certain circumstances, however, the names and context have been
altered to protect the identity of the people involved. Only
in those circumstances in which the personalities involved
are public figures have I retained their real names.

Library of Congress Catalog Card Number: 93-078998

ISBN 1-56977-600-8

10 9 8 7 6 5 4 3 2 1

First Edition

Printed in the United States of America

Faith, Joy, and Grace are their middle names,

Wife, Daughter, and Daughter are
their relationships to me.

From them I draw encouragement to write;

To them I dedicate the results of the writing.

Preface

The foreman of the jury stands to deliver the verdict. The judge, dressed in a black robe, asks, "How say you?" The foreman intones gravely. "We find the defendant GUILTY AS CHARGED. The convicted criminal slumps downward into a chair. He knows what the verdict means. It means punishment, it means pain, it means loss of personal freedom, it means grief.

Though we may not have stood in a court of law to hear such a statement of guilt pronounced upon us, we have all encountered the feeling of guilt in our souls. Guilt is like blood. If you're alive, it flows through the veins of your heart. You can't see guilt as you can see blood, but you can surely feel its pulse.

I don't know anyone who doesn't feel guilty at one time or another in life. Do you? If I ever meet a person who has never felt remorse, I will fear that person.

Have you ever felt guilty? Sure you have. You've wrestled with the conscience and battled the sense of remorse that threatens to leave you joyless and defeated. You've heard the awful words from within your own heart and from without, from the mouths of others.

We know what the declaration of guilt means. It means an end to joy; it means torment; it means hurt and personal agony.

Knowing that almost everyone has felt guilt and that guilt threatens to gnaw away the abundant life that God wants to give to each one of us, I believe we need to find ways to redemptively handle our remorse. I wrote this work precisely to offer help to those who want to understand guilt better and who want to find ways to learn its lessons of life.

Through a combination of biblical insight, personal stories, and historical and contemporary anecdotes, I have sought to lay out a clear understanding of what causes guilt and what we can do to relieve ourselves of the worst effects of it. Though guilt is almost inevitable (and is even sometimes helpful), it need not be destructive. We can accept the value of guilt without driving forever down the dead-end street of constant remorse.

On the last day of Jesus' life with us, He found Himself hanging between two guilty men. Below Him a crowd of guilty people milled about in the dust and heat. Each person in the scene, except Jesus, had reason for remorse. All of them, in their honest moments, felt the bondage of their individual sin.

As His breath became more shallow and His eyes began to dim, Jesus reared up for one more glorious moment. Like a benediction from Heaven He poured out the define offering: "Father, forgive them."

We don't know what happened with everyone in that crowd at the cross. Maybe they all heard the offer of forgiveness granted by Jesus. Maybe only a few heard it. In any event, the offer of Jesus still stands. It still stands because we're no different from the watching mob. Guilt continues to plague us.

Amazingly, though, God also continues to offer us forgiveness. The benediction still echoes from the hill.

GUILT. Each one has it.

FORGIVENESS. Each one needs it.

May this book help you admit the one so you can find the other.

Contents

THE GUILT TRIP

GETTING OFF A
DEAD-END STREET

I

All Blood Flows Red

The Universality of Guilt

The authorities found the remains of his body on March 30, 1987—within two miles of his home. A friend of mine from the police station called me with the news. "He was so close to his house, you'd think somebody could have helped him," said the officer.

Listening to the policeman's words, my thoughts skipped backward six months, to September 29, 1986, the day Ted disappeared, the day I went to meet him for lunch.

I rang the door bell of the red-brick ranch-style home for the third time, looking at my watch as I did so: 12:28. Ted had agreed to meet me at noon at his house. I had already waited in the car for twenty-five minutes, figuring that he was simply late for our appointment. Now though, I began to wonder if he had forgotten.

Peeking through the window (as we all do when we think someone is home but is not answering), I saw a black upright piano, a sofa and two wingback chairs sitting in the living room.

Though I rang the bell once more for good measure, I realized that Ted wasn't home. Normally, that wouldn't have bothered me. But this wasn't a typical lunch appointment. Instead, it was an appointment made out of a deep concern I had for Ted.

For several months I had counseled with him, seeking to help him overcome some unusual stresses at work and in his personal life. Recognizing a deep emotional trauma in him, which I as his pastor could not sufficiently handle, I had referred him to a psychiatrist in our community. The psychiatrist had assured me within the last week that Ted was making progress.

Yet, walking away from his house, my anxiety surfaced for several reasons. First, in spite of my attempts to talk him out of it, Ted had recently resigned his position on the public relations committee of the church. Also, in our private conversations, he demonstrated an increasingly weak sense of self-esteem.

Then, just yesterday, Sunday afternoon, I had received a phone call that turned up the heat under my concern for Ted.

Just finishing lunch and worn out from the Sunday service at church, I picked up the phone. I recognized the voice of Ted's wife.

"Dr. Parker," her timid voice said, "this is Linda Philips. I wanted to talk with you for a minute about Ted. He's really depressed. I don't know what I should do."

Having visited with Ted the past week, I wasn't surprised by her call. But, neither was I especially concerned about this most recent development. After all, he had exhibited the same despondency numerous times before this. Plus, the psychiatrist had assured me that Ted was getting stronger. My response demonstrated my outlook.

"Is it any worse than before?"

"No, I don't think so," she said. "I'm just at my wit's end to know what to do."

"Do you think I should come over?" Secretly, I hoped she would say no. I hadn't finished my study for the Sunday night sermon and knew I would be hard-pressed to get it completed if I spent much time talking to Ted.

"No, I just want you to pray for him. He just seems so down."

"Is he talking to you?"

"Yes, but he keeps saying he's no good to anyone, that he's a failure."

"Could I talk with him for a moment?"

A few seconds later Ted spoke, "Hello." His voice sounded flat, like a computerized answering machine.

"Ted? This is Gary. Linda tells me you're feeling down today?"

"Yeah, I guess so. Things just don't make much sense anymore."

"Could we get together tomorrow and talk about this?"

"I guess we could."

"Can I take you to lunch?"

"O.K."

"What about if I pick you up around noon at your house?"

"O.K."

"Good. Ted, could I talk with Linda for another moment please?"

Without another word, he turned over the phone.

"Gary, this is Linda again. Does he sound O.K. to you?"

Not able to discern much from his short statements, but having seen him depressed on other occasions, I answered. "He's obviously down, but he's been down lots of times before this. When did he last see Dr. Williams?"

"Just a few days ago. He said Ted seemed O.K."

"That's what he told me, too. Is he supposed to see him again this week?"

"I think so."

"Well, I'm going to meet Ted for lunch tomorrow. If he's not better by then, we'll get him to Dr. Williams earlier than his appointment. Does that sound O.K. to you?"

"Yeah, that sounds fine."

"O.K. then. I'll see him tomorrow. But, if you need me tonight, don't hesitate to call."

We hung up simultaneously.

That was yesterday. Now, as I stepped off the porch of Ted's home, a chill shot through me, in spite of the warmth of an early fall South Carolina sun. Trying not to surrender to the near-panic which I felt, I drove quickly back to the church and called Linda at work.

"Do you know where Ted might be?"

"Isn't he supposed to have lunch with you?"

"Yes, but I've just come from the house and

he wasn't there. Or at least he didn't come to the door."

I tried to remain calm. "Any idea where he might be?'

Linda stayed cool. "I haven't seen him since I left for work. He might have just forgotten."

Not sure where to go from there, I offered lamely, "I'm sure that's what happened."

Putting the phone down, I tried to focus on other matters. But thoughts of Ted kept creeping back into my head—worrisome thoughts—thoughts dark and sad. I feared the worst.

The days and months ahead proved my fears well-grounded. Never again would I hear Ted's voice. Never again would his wife hold him close. Never again would he sit to my right in the pew as a member of the congregation of worshippers I served as pastor. He disappeared. For almost six months his family, his church and his community searched for him, thinking they saw him, but being disappointed, hoping and praying that he would turn up again.

But that never happened. Instead, on March 30, 1987, an electrical company employee, cutting a path through the woods almost within yelling distance of Ted's house, found his remains—his death, the result of a suicide.

I'll never forget the rush of emotion that flooded my soul and my eyes when I heard the sad news. I would miss Ted, a friend who had given me old gospel albums from his collection to enjoy, a friend with whom I had played golf, a young man, my age, who had talent and humor and personality. But, Ted had given over to despair and chosen death over life.

Though I had suspected this for months as the family and I waited to learn his fate, I hoped and prayed that something else had happened, that he had simply fled from his problems, that he had suffered psychotic amnesia, or even that he had run off with another woman. I hoped anything, no matter how bizarre, in the effort to convince myself that the worst hadn't happened. But, of course, it had.

As the grief settled over me, an andiron heavy on my shoulders, I suddenly realized that another emotion also weighed down on me. I hadn't expected this one. But now it hit, a house-sized stone hurled at me, striking me square in the chest.

Though I tried to dodge it, I couldn't. I felt the sharp punch of GUILT knock the wind from my lungs. Guilt that I hadn't done more to help Ted. Guilt that I had failed him and his family. Guilt that I hadn't sufficiently ministered to him and his need.

I thought, "You should have known he was suicidal! You should have taken steps to prevent it. You should have ignored the psychiatrist who assured you that Ted was making progress. You should have stopped this!" The harsh clang of guilt stung my ears and crushed my spirit.

In the days and months that followed the discovery of Ted's body, I sought diligently to minister to his family. I performed his funeral. I maintained contact with his wife, two children, mom, and brothers. I encouraged them, visited with them, and, to the best of my ability, loved them. Yet, the sense of not doing enough, the shadow of guilt, still hung over me.

Years have now passed since Ted's death. Much has changed. But two things haven't. One, I still miss him as a friend. Two, I still deal with the guilt feeling that I didn't do enough to help him through his emotional and spiritual wasteland.

Looking back now, I recognize that I wasn't the only one who experienced guilt feelings as the result of Ted's tragic end. In fact, at least two of his friends and one of his family members spoke to me later of their concern that they had failed to encourage him enough. Apparently, guilt struck many, if not most, of the people who knew him and tried to care for him.

As I continue to grow as a minister and a Christian, I have discovered that we don't have to endure such a tragedy as a suicide in order to feel guilt. Instead, guilt plagues almost every one of us at one point or another.

The guilt can arise out of circumstances like those between Ted, his family, and me. Or, they can arise out of more normal situations. A husband stays at work past nine P.M. and doesn't get home in time to see much of his wife and either of his two preschool children before they go to bed. Guilt tugs at his heart as he wonders what kind of father or husband he is.

A mother takes a job to help the family make financial ends meet. To accept that job she has to leave her four-year-old in day care. Guilt chews her up, telling her she's not a good mother.

A teenager drinks three beers on Friday

night after the football game against the express wishes of her mom and dad, who have warned of the evils of alcohol all her life. Guilt goes down with the beer, flooding her insides as the beer fills her up.

A ten-year-old, afraid of failing a test, scans the paper of a friend in the next desk, stealing the answers. He passes the test, but not the court of his conscience, which tells him he's a bad boy.

In a thousand ways and in a million circumstances, we face the grim visage of guilt.

In their work *Guilt Free: The Life You Deserve to Live,* Paula and Dick McDonald, psychologists and authors, relate a number of situations and circumstances in which people find themselves struggling with their feelings of remorse. After considering the entire spectrum of life, the McDonalds reach the conclusion: "Everybody did feel guilt—in some ways, at sometimes." Thus, they conclude, guilt is "universal."

Most Americans remember *The Bridge on the River Kwai.* That movie and the book that preceded it told the story of a daring effort by American and British troops in World War II to destroy a key bridge connecting a vital supply line of the Japanese Army in Indochina.

Though dramatic, neither the book nor the movie related what really happened during World War II in the Thailand jungle of Kanchanaburi. To get the real story we have to listen to the people who actually lived through this heartrending drama of suffering and death.

One such man, seventy-two-year-old Takashi Nagase, an intelligence officer with the Imperial Japanese Army that oversaw the construction of the railroad (known as the "Death Railway") from Bangkok to Rangoon, witnessed scores of hideous acts of cruelty. The Japanese soldiers heaped humiliation and deprivation upon the thousands of Allied prisoners who worked as slaves to build the railroad and the bridge over the river.

Nagase watched decent Japanese men turned into barbarous tyrants under the stresses and fears of war. He saw them resort to violence and hatred as they oversaw the work of the unfortunate Allied troops as they built the 258 miles of rail through the sunburned tropical forest. He watched himself descend into attitudes and activities he would typically have rejected as uncivilized. Under the harsh hands of Japanese soldiers, 16,000 prisoners died through starvation or execution.

Surviving the war, Nagase returned to Japan and sought to rebuild his ravaged country. Unfortunately for him, rebuilding Japan was easier than rebuilding his life. He found that physical survival didn't necessarily mean emotional and spiritual well-being. In fact, as the years passed, he increasingly found himself facing the ghosts of those prisoners who had suffered and died during the construction of the Kwai River Bridge. Those ghosts kept him from any sense of peace. They inhabited his mind and heart, always pointing to him as a criminal and a brute.

Two decades after coming home from the jungle, Nagase decided he had to do something to lay those ghosts to rest. In 1963, he returned to Kanchanaburi to face his tormentors. He walked to the Allied cemetery near the site of the Kwai River Bridge to make his peace with his past. There, with trembling hands and a hopeful heart, he laid a wreath on one of the graves.

Fortunately for his spirit, his act of contrition and acknowledgment worked. He walked away from the grave of Kanchanaburi a free man. With the wreath, Nagase also laid down his guilt. As he later described the feelings of release that washed over him, "The history of the atrocities cannot be erased. All Japanese are born guilty. The sin flows in our blood."

In reality, Nagase speaks for all of us. Though we didn't all participate in the crimes of the Japanese, we've all participated in "crimes" against other people; we've all failed in one way or another; we've all succumbed to selfishness, to pride, to greed, to anger, to lust, to deceit, to hypocrisy, to self-righteousness. Truly, when we're honest, we admit we have seen the enemy, and he is us. We cannot deny our transgressions and we cannot avoid the guilt our transgressions have created.

The sin flows in our blood.

II

A Fence and a Sign
A Definition of Guilt

Carroll Campbell, the governor of South Carolina, stood before the congregation gathered at Trinity Episcopal Cathedral in Columbia, SC. He looked out at the packed crowd, many of them with eyes red from crying. Campbell delivered no political speech today. Instead, he spoke words of eulogy for Lee Atwater, the guitar-pickin' South Carolina boy who had risen through the ranks of the Republican party to become the campaign manager for President George Bush and the head of the GOP.

On the way to the top Atwater had made scores of political enemies. Known for his pit-bull style of campaigning, Atwater yielded no quarter and asked for none. For him, only victory counted. It wasn't how you played the game, but whether you won or lost that mattered. Atwater had never lost—until now. But, he couldn't out-campaign death. Cancer swamped him in the final poll.

His eyes glistening with emotion, Governor Campbell spoke of Atwater's last days fighting the ravages of cancer and the demons of a troubled conscience. "Over the last year, during this most important campaign that he ever ran, Lee may have grown the most. Lee won that campaign. He was at peace with himself, at peace with his fellow man and at peace with his God."

The somber-suited congregation nodded as Campbell spoke. They had read the newspaper accounts. They had heard the stories.

Atwater had experienced a spiritual and emotional transformation in the last year of his life. He had called old enemies to apologize. He had expressed regret and remorse to a number of his former political opponents for his intemperate remarks made in the heat of past political battles. Lee Atwater had admitted mistakes and sought absolution of them.

Reading the obituaries, I couldn't help but wonder, "What caused him to act this way before he died?" I can imagine only one answer. Atwater discovered more than cancer chewing on his insides in his last year. He also discovered guilt. Then, just as he sought a cure for the disease of his body, he also sought a cure for the disease of his soul. He sought to cleanse himself of guilt before he died.

Everyone experiences guilt. To support that statement, I want to define what I mean by "guilt." After all, before I can say that everyone experiences something, it will help if we can agree upon what that experience is. To define guilt I want to use the experience of Lee Atwater as a parable of the remorse that does, indeed, strike us all.

Guilt Is a Feeling

Guilt is a painful feeling of self reproach resulting from a belief that one has done something wrong or immoral. In this definition I hear three key concepts.

First, it says guilt is a "painful feeling of self reproach." Notice it doesn't say guilt is the "act" itself. An act may cause us to experience guilt, but it stands prior to any thought, feeling, or spiritual unease that results.

Guilt remains behind the event that created

it. Guilt is the ash left the day after a fire burns down a house. It is the white-hot, radioactive rubbish generated by nuclear fission. Guilt lives as the unsettled anxiety in the life that has broken its moral code.

Guilt exists as a mental, emotional, and spiritual disharmony within us that we feel when we have broken a personal morality or have violated a cherished value.

Obviously, Lee Atwater suffered so long from this disharmony that it drove him to make his peace with himself, with others and with his God before his death. He suffered from this unrest until he found a way to free himself from it just prior to his death.

Rights and Wrongs Do Exist

The second part of our definition holds that guilt results from a belief that one has done something wrong or immoral. Obviously, to believe that we've done something wrong means that we have to accept certain standards of conduct as appropriate and others as inappropriate. Although a small percentage of people seem to have lost the capacity to distinguish between right and wrong, the vast majority of the human race acknowledges the reality that some actions are inappropriate and others are acceptable. Atwater knew this before he discovered his cancer. If he had known no moral standards, if he had possessed no sense of good and bad, correct or incorrect behavior, then he would never have felt a compunction to make the apologies he made. To feel guilt requires us to believe in certain moral codes.

For centuries, theologians and philosophers have debated whether such knowledge of a moral code arrives prepackaged with the child at birth or whether each person learns it through societal adaptation. Immanuel Kant, the eighteenth-century German philosopher, spoke of the "oughtness" that every person innately feels; C.S. Lewis, the Anglican teacher and author described the "Law of Human Nature" as the built-in guide to good and bad behavior. On the other hand, the father of modern psychology, Sigmund Freud led the parade of those who said that distinctions between right and wrong come from environmental circumstances. We cannot settle the issue of the source of the sense of right and wrong here. At this juncture, let us simply accept the result without delving into the origins. Guilt means that we each can develop and have developed internal values that we can and do violate.

Obviously, we can possess distorted and confused values. We can feel guilt for something we do or don't do that no one else will recognize as a valid reason for our unease. Guilt can result from legitimate or illegitimate reasons. For example, a wife might experience remorse because she was visiting her parents out-of-state when her supposedly healthy husband died of a heart attack. Though she couldn't know that would happen and couldn't have prevented it if she had, she might suffer guilt anyway. Though I will consider both legitimate and illegitimate guilt in more depth later in this book, let me note here that the two types do exist, and we often find it difficult to discern between them. We should also recognize that our individual values might not find agreement with everyone else's. We might declare an action right, and someone else might see it entirely differently. Our perspectives determine how we view each event of life.

A story illustrates this difference of perspective well. A middle-aged black doorman working at an upscale hotel in New York heroically throws himself into the path of an oncoming bus in a successful effort to save the life of a six-year-old white girl who had stepped in front of it. After the doorman stops shaking, he finds himself surrounded by people with a variety of responses to his actions.

His wife shouts, "You fool, you could have been killed saving that child, and then your own children wouldn't have had a father to care for them."

His brother criticizes him also. "If you're going to kill yourself, don't do it for a white child."

The hotel owner calls it a "selfless act" and gives the man a bonus.

The girl's parents, of course, hail the doorman as a hero.

We do own our unique perspectives on what we see as right and wrong, don't we? The same event can trigger a host of interpretations. In effect, we each live with our own list of "shoulds" and "should nots." We keep in the pockets of our hearts the charts with our rights and wrongs enumerated there.

Regardless of the fact that we see events differently, almost all of us do posses the capacity to believe in a good and a bad.

We Can and Do Know
These Rights and Wrongs

A third aspect of our definition of guilt tells us we have to be able to perceive we've violated the standard we espouse before we experience remorse. If Atwater had never understood that his previous statements about other politicians could have hurt them and him, then he could not have stood accountable or responsible for his actions.

If a person has no mental capacity to recognize wrong from right then society cannot and does not hold them accountable for crimes they commit against themselves or others. The insanity plea and retardation plea in our system of justice protect those who cannot make the distinction between what a society allows or doesn't allow. Though we often say, "ignorance is no defense," that doesn't apply to personal, state, or religious standards of thought and action. In these cases, ignorance is a defense, a legally accepted one when the person has no capacity to understand the charges brought to bear.

Let me make this clearer with an illustration. Recently, I accompanied a good friend of

mine into the woods to deer hunt. The pre-
dawn air bit sharply at my face as I sat high in
the crook of the branches of a towering oak,
hoping and praying that a deer would appear—
and fast at that! Unfortunately, none did. We
crouched in our cramped quarters, blowing
silently on our frozen hands, talking only in
whispers as hour after hour passed. Though we
waited patiently, nothing happened, and the
sun, gradually rising added almost no heat to
the early winter air.

Finally we gave up and climbed out of the
tree. Wanting to get back to the truck as soon
as possible, I suggested, "Let's cut through the
woods instead of taking the road back." Chip
agreed. Almost running, we hustled across the
unfamiliar territory, anticipating the warmth of
the truck heater.

Within a half mile of the deer stand, we
crashed through the undergrowth and came to a
broken down, rusty fence. Though we weren't
sure who owned the property beyond the fence,
we didn't hesitate. Instead, we climbed through
the barbed wire and trudged ahead.

Suddenly, we heard the leaves crackle to our
left. Both of us froze—maybe a deer was
approaching! No, it wasn't a deer. Instead, a

bearded giant wearing bib overalls and toting a shotgun over his left shoulder pushed his way toward us. Sizing us up, he grunted, "Don't you guys know you're trespassing?"

Apologetically, I said, "No sir, we didn't."

Chip added, "We saw the fence but we didn't see any sign warning us against trespassing. So, we thought it would be O.K."

Our accuser spat out a stream of chewing tobacco that landed just short of our feet. "Guess I'll have to get me a sign then," he said as he turned and walked away.

This grizzled hunter and owner of the land understood a reality that comes into play whenever we speak of guilt as a universal phenomenon. For anyone to feel guilt, that person must have both a "fence" (a code of conduct) and a "sign" (an understandable warning) that shows where the forbidden land actually begins and warns each person not to cross it.

Without knowing the rules, you can't know what to do or not to do. If we possess no known standard, we can't be held accountable for it. Unless we tell the child not to mark the wall with crayons, we should feel no surprise when the child does precisely that.

A known standard enables us to act correctly or incorrectly and to experience the remorse of guilt. Obviously, most of us can know the difference between acceptable and unacceptable conduct. We can know it because the mind (the intellect) and the heart (the emotional self), combined in the conscience, create the awareness in us. Guilt begins when we see we've crossed the line between the two. Another person can tell us we should feel guilty, but that won't create the emotion in us unless we believe it for ourselves.

An Authority Exists to Determine Rights and Wrongs

Guilt implies not only internal standards, but also an authority (or a group of authorities) who help us determine those standards.

Risking the possibility of being labeled a chauvinist, I want to relate the story of a man who dreamed that he had died and now stood at the gates of heaven. Gazing overhead, he saw two entrances to the heavenly city. Above one entrance, he read this sign: "All henpecked husbands stand in this line." Billions of men stood in that line. It stretched for miles past the horizon.

Above the second entrance, he read this sign: "All husbands who are not henpecked stand in this line." One lone male stood there.

Intrigued, the dreamer walked over to the lone man and asked him: "Why are you standing in this line?" The man shrugged his shoulders and said: "Because my wife told me to stand here, that's why!"

This lone man had learned a lesson all of us, regardless of gender, learn quickly. We live with "authorities" who tell us what we should and shouldn't do. We live with "authorities" who tell us what's right and wrong.

Standards Not Necessarily Religious

When I say that everyone feels guilty at some point in life, I'm making the claim that guilt is not exclusively a religious term. Instead, the term refers to the realization that every person—atheist, agnostic, and devout believer alike—has crossed the line of their own code of conduct. Indeed, I'm saying that every person, religious or not, has such a code constructed.

The definition of guilt used earlier and those typically applied by the secular psychologist never refer to any necessary divine origin of remorse. Anyone, regardless of religious inclination or the lack thereof, will fit under these definitions. Yet, all say the guilt response begins because the person believes that they have "done something wrong" or have "fallen short of the ideal."

In secular terms, we label these wrongs "mistakes, errors, failures or shortcomings." When we do put this in religious terminology we call it sin.

Though the standards we accept don't necessarily find their origin in any conscious religious context, we typically discover that they lead us, at some point, to a contact with spiritual issues. Dr. Paul Tournier, the noted Swiss author, therapist, and theologian, once said, "We cannot tackle the problem of guilt without dealing with the religious questions which it poses."

When we speak of guilt, we inevitably find ourselves at the heart of Judeo-Christian theology. In fact, we find ourselves at the heart of almost every theology. From the earliest religious artifacts, archaeologists have found evidence of the belief that each person inevitably falls short of the standards they hold dear and suffer guilt as the result.

In ancient Egyptian literature of 2400 B.C., writings indicated that moral transgressions angered the sun god, Re. In Mesopotamia, called the birthplace of civilization, sin was seen as an offense against the sensibilities of the fertility gods. In China, even prior to Confucius, people said sin upset the cosmic order ordained by the Will of Heaven. The words *tsui, o,* and *kuo* came to symbolize "evil," "bad," and to "overstep the mark." The Hindu faith calls sin "ignorance" and finds its result in moral wrongdoing. The Islamic tradition sees humans as weaklings who fall to the temptation of sin and commit acts that require forgiveness and cleansing.

The Judeo-Christian Scripture describes sin in at least five ways.

First, it refers to sin as a "deviation from what is good and right."

It speaks second, of "missing the mark," as in firing an arrow and not hitting the target.

In other biblical passages, the word *sin* refers not just to missing the mark, but to "overstepping the boundaries." We see the picture of a person stepping over the line drawn in the sand that they have been ordered not to cross.

A fourth form of the word means "erring through ignorance." A person fails to do what they should because they know no better.

Perhaps the most profound term used to define sin speaks of it as "defiance against God." This usage describes the human being as a rebel not only against society, but also against the Almighty. Thus sin exists as more than a failure or a mistake. It is willful disobedience of a divine standard.

Not too long ago my youngest daughter, Ashley Grace, decided to redecorate the walls of her bedroom. Unfortunately, at three years of age, she used a crayon to do it. As I entered the room I saw the markings she had made and ordered her to stop. She glowered at me and said, "I can do it if I want."

"You can do it if you want to, but I will spank you if you do. You get to choose which it will be."

She stared at me for another moment, then put the crayon down. Thankfully, she chose not to disobey.

At other times, though, she has disobeyed me—just as I once disobeyed my parents. In similar fashion, all of us have chosen at times to deliberately defy the will of our God as we know it, expressed to us either in Scripture, in prayer, or in our conscience. That's the meaning of sin many of us recognize. Such transgressions against our God or against another person spawn guilt.

I know we don't like to look at these concepts. It hurts us to admit that we fail in our relationship to our God and in our relationships to other people. Yet, honesty demands that we admit our spiritual waywardness. We see, then, that committing a wrong does not necessarily relate to the concept of a deity. It could, but it doesn't have to do so.

Let's recap our definition of guilt. Guilt is the mental, emotional, and potentially spiritual anxiety we feel when we perceive that we have broken some self-proscribed or other standard of ethic and activity. It lives as a feeling that we "should have" responded differently, that we failed to think or act correctly, that another course of action would have been better for us or for others. It results from our real or imagined transgressions (also called "sins") against our inner code.

At the beginning of this chapter I recounted the story of Lee Atwater. He experienced the disharmony of guilt. Thankfully, he found a way beyond it before he died. Hopefully, we can find a way beyond our guilt while we yet live. To do so, we need to begin by understanding the authority figures that create guilt in us.

III

A Bony Finger

The Creators of Guilt

In Karl Menninger's much-quoted book, *Whatever Became of Sin?* he describes the following scene:

> *On a sunny day in September, 1972, a stern-faced, plainly dressed man could be seen standing still on a street corner in the busy Chicago Loop. As pedestrians hurried by on their way to lunch or business, he would solemnly lift his right arm, and pointing to the person nearest him, intone loudly the single word, "GUILTY!" Then, without any change of expression, he would resume his stiff stance for a few moments before repeating the gesture.*

35

Menninger's image reminds us the guilt we experience (whether legitimate or not) arises because *we find ourselves facing the accusing finger of a variety of authorities which point to us and declare us "GUILTY"!* In the last chapter we accepted this reality without identifying the sources of the accusations that create guilt within us. Now, however, I want to identify the "bony fingers" that condemn us so readily. Only after we've identified our accusers can we begin to oppose them.

Ancestral Accusers

Within the cultures that civilization has known through the ages, certain actions have been universally condemned. Stealing, for example, has been unacceptable in every culture since the dawn of time. Although we cannot conclusively determine the origin of such universal strictures, the philosopher and psychologist, Carl Jung suggests we have within us a "collective unconscious" that helps govern the actions we take.

Speaking of this "collective unconscious," Jung said, "Our mind has a history....For, though a child is not born conscious, his mind is not a tabula rasa....It has been built up in the course of millions of years and represents a history of which it is the result." In other words, said Jung, from the moment we push forward from the womb we possess a type of universal knowledge of what is right and what is wrong. Our ancestor's basic social norms have ingrained themselves over time in the subconscious mind of every one of us. These "racial archetypes," as Jung called them, become sources for determining our values. We would experience these restraints even if our parents never taught them to us.

Jung's concepts were preceded by almost two millennia in a letter by the Jewish rabbi turned Christian believer, Paul of Tarsus, to the church at Rome.

> *When the Gentiles, who do not have the law do instinctively the things of the law, these not having the law, are a law unto themselves, in that they show the work of the law written in their hearts, their conscience bearing them witness, and their thoughts alternately accusing or defending them.* (Romans 2:14-15)

Though Paul had never heard of Carl Jung and though the two might argue over the creative origin of this innate sense of right and wrong, he apparently agreed with the psychologist! Paul said each of us lives with a "law written in our hearts" that either accuses or defends us. This "law," generated either by a combination of the past histories of our society or by the divine "ought" (or a combination of the two) and governed by the present watchful eyes of the conscience and the community of which we're a part, continues to accuse us of crimes or acquit us of the charges.

So, when we transgress one of these internal barriers, given to us by our shared humanity, the accusing finger of guilt points at us and causes an emotional unrest in our spirits.

Internal Accusers

Sigmund Freud, the father of modern psychoanalytical thought, believed the sense of guilt was the most important problem in the evolution of culture." Given his profound interest in the subject, Freud sought to uncover the psychological mechanism that triggered the feeling in the human personality. To do this,

Freud developed the concept of the "id," the "ego," and the "superego." In this theory, the id represents the most basic drive of the personality—the natural, instinctive part of the self that pursues, without conscience, what it wants. The id represents the personality at its animalistic base.

Understandably, we can't allow the id to run amuck without restraint. So, to serve as the policeman for the id, our personality includes the superego. The superego represents the internal, cultural restrictions placed on each of us so we can work and live in harmony with one another. It serves as the fence that keeps us out of areas of conduct we shouldn't cross. It acts as the internal censor to control the id and keep it at bay. The superego gives birth to what we call the conscience.

Standing between the id, which seeks total freedom, and the superego, which binds the id in the straightjacket of society's norms, we find the ego. It serves the total self, working to balance the drives of the id and the restraints of the superego.

To say it in understandable language, the id represents the wild animal in all of us; the superego represents the fences or cages to keep the wild animal at bay; and the ego represents the national park where the wild animal can roam, bounded by fences, without hurting itself or anyone else. The animal lives with restrictions, but with those that allow freedom without danger. In the healthy personality, these three parts find a balance between unlimited freedom and imprisoning restraint.

In Freud's theory, and modern psychology has largely accepted it, the superego, also called the conscience, lives as the guilt-producing aspect in each person. It lies like a coiled snake with fangs bared, ready to strike at the moment of our real or perceived failures. We see the conscience as our first judge, prepared to pronounce us guilty if and when we transgress our internal values.

Relational Accusers

Parent to Child Guilt

Several years ago a seminary friend of mine sat up with me into the wee hours of the morning. As we talked, he poured out his hurt. Though studying for a divinity degree, he felt a profound sense of unworthiness for Christian service. Disconsolate over an inability to overcome his self-reproach, he openly shared his torment. This is his story.

He was seven years old. One rainy day in April his father, an abusive alcoholic, went on one of his biannual binges. Tragically for my friend, he was the only one home when his drunken father staggered through the door. Entering the house, the father demanded to know where his wife was. The seven-year-old fearfully mumbled he didn't know. The father went into a curse-filled rage. Referring to the absent wife, the father castigated the boy for being her son. He cursed him for not knowing where she was. In words no child should hear, the father bellowed: "She's a bitch! And you're a son of a bitch!" With that the father turned and walked out of the house, leaving the crying child to deal with his shattered self.

That youngster grew up, embraced Christian faith, and entered the seminary, preparing to serve the church. Now, he sat across from me at 2 A.M.: "I've replayed my father's words over a million times in the last twenty years. Somehow, I internalized them and began to believe they were true. He made me feel guilty for even being alive. If I'm what he said I am, then I have no right to even think of serving God."

Thankfully, many of us have never faced this kind of verbal abuse from our parents. Yet, we do find ourselves living with the words of our parents reverberating in our hearts. We still see the standards of our parents pointing their fingers at us, telling us who we are and how we should act. We still tend to believe anything different from their standard is wrong.

The religious person finds numerous injunctions upholding the right of the parent to serve as the final authority for the child. The fifth commandment of the Jewish and Christian scriptures reminds us, "Honor your father and your mother so that your days may be prolonged in the land which the Lord your God gives to you." The New Testament reaffirms this. "Obey your parents in the Lord, for this is right" (Ephesians 6:1). When we ignore or deliberately choose a way different from the one our parents offer to us, we generally feel the twinge of guilt.

Even if we're not religiously inclined, the pattern holds true. Typically, the scenario works like this. Our parents ask us to act in certain ways, to limit ourselves in specific areas, to follow their leadership in a variety of circumstances. These parental injunctions relate to the friends we enjoy, the hours we keep, the studies we pursue in college, the mates we choose to marry, the careers we accept, and the places we live. No matter our age, our parents can find some aspect of life through which to exercise some control. Sometimes we obey and sometimes we don't. Even when we do obey, but wish we hadn't, and especially when we don't obey, we find ourselves at odds with the very powerful authority figure of our parents.

Typically, at some point, we will grow angry with them for establishing the standards and for calling for the obedience. Unfortunately, our anger doesn't alleviate the unrest we feel within ourselves. Instead, we feel the anger dissolving into guilt that we could even feel such hostility toward our loved ones. We face guilt over breaking the parental rule, plus guilt over getting angry at our parents who create them.

Child to Parent Guilt

In a humorous article from the *Kansas City Star,* Kathleen Parker writes of her experience at a recent Cub Scout meeting she attended with her son. Patting herself on the back for attending the meeting at the conclusion of a tough day, she unexpectedly found herself being castigated by the scoutmasters for not accepting a role as a leader in the organization. Under the guilt gun with the other parents to serve as scout leaders, she later wrote: "Here we were expecting to be rewarded for showing up. Instead, we are reminded that we are, in fact, pretty lousy parents."

If anyone can pull our guilt cord quicker than our own parents, it's our children. When we don't get home before they go to bed at night, we feel the tug. When we don't make enough money to provide them with tennis and piano and golf and dance; when we don't read to them every night like the really good parents do; when we miss their school play—all of this and more creates a seemingly no-win situation for the parent.

In the Old Testament Scriptures the writers recorded for us the discouraging events which surrounded the life of a Jewish patriarch and priest named Eli, who fathered two useless boys. The sons, Hophni and Phineas, lived lives unworthy of their father or their God. The

Scriptures say it this way: "The sons of Eli were worthless men." What tragic words— words that no parent wants inscribed over the lives of their children. Yet, parents live with constant fear that somehow, their children will turn out poorly, and they will shoulder most of the blame.

In 1983, the community of Warrenton, North Carolina, where I pastored, found itself the center of national attention. Four convicted murderers escaped from a maximum security prison in Virginia, fled down interstate 85 and ended up trapped in our isolated town of 2,500 people. Hundreds of highway patrolmen and national guardsmen swamped our hamlet, searching for the criminals. Unfortunately for us, the murderers remained hidden.

For weeks we were on edge, not knowing where or when the dangerous convicts would strike. During those tense days, hordes of television and newspaper media descended upon us. The reporters stuck microphones and cameras everywhere, into everyone's faces, hoping to catch the exploitable emotions of fear or anger for their viewers.

One night, worn out from the day's rapid events, I plopped down on the sofa to watch the latest news updates. The reporter I saw on the screen was sitting too, in a rocking chair, interviewing an obviously distraught woman.

It didn't take me long to figure it out. The reporter had found the mother of one of the murderers. He asked her inane questions. "Has your son contacted you?" "No," she said, tears on her cheeks. "Do you know where he might be?" "No." He pushed the microphone closer. "Can you tell us what happened to your son that caused him to turn to crime?" The tragic woman went limp as she mouthed the words, "Somewhere I let him down. Somehow I let him down."

Blaming herself for her son's crimes, she portrayed a painful example of the guilt that a child can impose upon a parent.

Spouse to Spouse Guilt

In the little classic *Letters to Philip* by Charlie Shedd, we read of a woman who suffered a car accident. She called her husband as soon as she could to tell him.

Seemingly oblivious to her condition, he asked, "How much damage did you do to the car?" His second words were, "Whose fault was it?"

Following this, he suggested, "Listen, darling, don't admit a thing! You call the insurance company and I'll call the lawyer. We can beat this thing."

His wife said little until this point. Then, she asked, "Well do you have any more instructions or questions?"

"No, I think that about covers it."

"Oh, does it?" she fumed. "In case you're interested, I'm at the hospital with five broken ribs."

I'm glad I wasn't that husband. He had to deal not only with his wife's anger, but also with his own guilt. How insensitive we can be to those we love the most. How unthinking!

Yet, we all—husbands and wives—have found ourselves acting in similar ways. When we do, when we fail our spouse in one way or another, we inevitably feel guilt.

The first weekend after my wife Melody and I returned from our honeymoon (over ten years ago now) I received an invitation to play golf. Without thinking about my wife's plans, I quickly accepted.

Saturday morning, I pulled out my clubs and started cleaning them. Watching me, Melody asked, "Where are you going?"

"Robert asked me to play golf."

Her lower lip dropped. "And you accepted without asking me?"

"Yes, I did."

She didn't say anything else. But, I could see her disappointment. Needless to say, I didn't enjoy my golf game. I felt guilty all day, thinking I had offended my new bride.

No matter how hard we try to avoid it, we will offend our mates. Our offenses will inevitably create the residue of guilt.

Friend to Friend

Have you ever made, then forgotten an appointment with a friend? Did you or your spouse or child ever receive a promotion or a pay raise or some distinguished honor or reward while your friend's family didn't? Have you ever opened a Christmas present from a friend and realized you had bought them nothing? If anything like this has happened to you, then you know friendship can create guilt.

Roger, a cherished friend of mine once told me this story. Though married for thirty-five years, he and his wife had never had an opportunity for a honeymoon. After the four children were born and his business had blossomed, he could never find the time. In fact, he and Rachael had never even taken a vacation alone.

In the summer of their thirty-fifth year, Roger changed all that. He took his wife to Hawaii. They spent an entire month sunning and sightseeing, eating and talking, swimming and relaxing—enjoying the rewards of a life of hard work.

The day he returned to his home in Greenville, South Carolina, the phone rang. His best friend was on the other end. He said, "Roger, this is Tom. I wanted you to hear this from me. I'm getting a divorce."

Roger was stunned. All he could think to say was, "I'm sorry."

"I know. I just wish you had been here four weeks ago. I've really needed you. But you weren't here."

No, Roger wasn't there. His absence created the presence of guilt because his friend poured the hot coals of blame upon him.

You forget to call on your friend's birthday; you make a friend a promise but circumstances interfere and you break it; you inadvertently break a confidence of a friend; you get angry at a friend's attitude and say something unkind.

You've discovered that relationships bring failures and failures bring guilt.

Establishment Accusers

I'll never forget the most embarrassing moment of my life. I was in the seventh grade at Northside Junior High, in Greenwood, South Carolina. My history teacher, a tiny woman, standing barely five feet tall, instructed my classmates and me to take our most recent test home and get our parents to sign it. Dutifully, I took my test (I made a 91) home to my Mom and Dad. Carelessly, however, I forgot to get their signature.

Upon arrival at school, I discovered my oversight. I had a choice to make. I could take the zero Mrs. Razier gave us when we didn't get our papers signed, or I could try to forge a signature.

Not believing Mrs. Razier would notice the forgery, I wrote "Mr. C. E. Parker" on the top, right-hand corner of the page.

Mrs. Razier was smarter than I thought. Right after lunch, she called me to her desk. "Did your Dad sign this paper, Gary?"

I thought about lying, but decided I better not add to my crime sheet. "No, Ma'am," I said. "I did."

She looked at me, hard. She said: "Here's what you've got to do. At the end of class today I want you to stand up before the class and tell everyone what you did." I went back to my desk, crestfallen, dreading the death sentence hanging over me. At 3 P.M. I walked to the front of the room and, red-faced, admitted my guilt.

That experience taught me a lesson. Every one of us has to deal with authority figures who demand obedience to certain standards of conduct. When we fail to obey we will come face-to-face with the possibility of guilt.

All of us come into contact with a variety of people who influence our circumstances. These "establishment influencers" (school teachers, coaches, fellow workers, mentors, government figures, etc.) bring a significant weight to bear in our lives as we listen to them and learn from them. They bring the power to create standards and, therefore, to create guilt, into our lives.

Whether it's a coach demanding a weight-lifting program in the off-season, a president calling us to involuntarily serve in the armed forces, a policeman directing us to stay under the speed limit, or a company president urging us to work seventy hours a week to make a larger profit for the firm, we all come into contact with people who create certain standards they want us to follow. If and when we choose not to follow those standards, the potential for guilt raises its insistent head.

Religious Accusers

No creator of guilt jabs us as insistently as the divine accuser, who pokes at our failures and calls them sin. For most of us, the notion we've failed to uphold the standards of our God, whether Christian or non-Christian, acts as the first source of personal guilt.

Harvard psychologist Robert Coles relates the experience that alerted him to the power of religious guilt in people. A woman, overwhelmed by guilt, came to him for help for her unending depression. In the interview, she poured out her story. She had committed adultery, and her remorse threatened to destroy her. Coles suggested that her guilt was based on the connection she made in her emotions between her lover and her father. The woman disagreed. She said, "You keep trying to find the cause of my difficulty within me. But I believe there's someone else who has to be mentioned."

"Who?"

"God."

He countered by saying her psychic pain over her immorality had led her to express herself in unnecessarily religious terms. She persisted in her feelings, not willing to accept a purely psychological explanation of her anxiety. She concluded, "God's judgment matters more than my own."

Many of us find ourselves responding in a similar manner. We believe God's judgment matters. Our religious sensitivity heightens our sense of guilt because we perceive moral issues in more than human terms. We believe our transgressions at times break divine standards.

Obviously, our consideration of divine standards of morality can lead to all sorts of unhealthy reactions. We confuse and distort God's desires for our lives and end up suffering from unnecessary and misguided remorse. Even with the negative possibilities, however, we dare not ignore the divine word of good and evil.

In a profound encounter between Nathan, a guarded prophet and David, the king of Israel, we see a classic example of the divine standard conflicting with a human transgression.

Many of us know the background of this story. For those who don't, this episode capped a series of despicable actions of David, ruler of Israel. As king, David possessed the right to choose almost anyone as his wife. The only women beyond his legal and moral reach were those already married. His religion wouldn't allow adultery.

David, however, stepped outside the boundaries of his religious law and committed rape upon Bathsheba, the wife of Uriah, one of his loyal soldiers. Then, to hide his act, David sent Uriah to the front of a fierce battle. As planned, Uriah died in the conflict and never discovered the unfaithfulness of his wife with David.

David, however, didn't escape from his deed. Nathan, the prophet, brought it home to him in dramatic fashion. He told the king the following parable.

Once there were two men, one rich and the other poor. The poor man owned one little lamb. He and his family loved the lamb as a pet. They nurtured it like a child. Then, sadly, the rich man, who had many lambs, took the one lamb from the poor man and his family.

Upon hearing the story, David bellowed, "As the LORD lives, the man who has done this deserves to die."

"You are the man."

The words of Nathan instantly pierced the heart of David. We hear his simple, but profound recognition of his guilt. David said to Nathan, "I have sinned against the Lord" (2 Samuel 12).

Having broken the commandment of God, David now faced the accusing finger of the courageous prophet. Through Nathan's thunderous words, "Thou art the man," David also faced his own guilt.

Though not *all* of us believe in a godly standard, many do find ourselves facing what we see as a number of divine absolutes in life. Sometimes we discover the divine standard in our understanding of the Scriptures. At other moments, we accept the words of a preacher, rabbi, or priest who castigates us for our spiritual and moral shortcomings. In other circumstances, a fellow layperson serves as the mediator of what is and is not appropriate to godliness. Even people who have largely rejected any formal expression of religion still find themselves dealing with the moralities they learned in childhood.

Of all the creators of guilt, none exercises the power over us that religion does. The guilt that the conscience produces, the guilt that parents can induce, and much of the guilt that the establishment creates derive their ultimate power from divine authorities.

IV

Ghosts and Guilt

The Destructive Power of Guilt

386. That's the number of North Vietnamese soldiers that war hero Mike Hall believed he killed during a frenzied battle on February 26, 1971. The Viet Cong had attacked the hill where Hall's outfit was stationed. Heavily outnumbered, Hall's unit seemed doomed to complete annihilation. Gunfire and grenades exploded all around him as he tried to fight off the hordes of green-clad enemy. In the heat of the action, Hall grabbed the controls of a twin forty-millimeter artillery piece called the "Duster." Swinging it around, he poured its immense firepower into the onrushing enemy. Scores of them fell instantly, stacking up like cordwood, dead and dying. Hall and a few of his buddies survived.

After the smoke cleared, the body count

revealed 386 men dead in Hall's line of fire. A scared man defending his fellow soldiers and himself, Hall had acted heroically in the eyes of his fellow soldiers. Unfortunately, Hall's choice of weapons created a problem.

Upon review of the battle, Hall's company commander told him it was against the Geneva Convention to use "The Duster"—an anti-aircraft weapon—against ground troops. Then, to protect Hall against possible court-martial, the officer called in an air strike against dead North Vietnamese. He officially attributed the death total to an attack by air power.

Hall finished out his tour of duty like the good soldier he was and returned as a hero to his native Minnesota after his time ended. He wore a Bronze Star on his shirt, a decoration for his bravery. Sadly, he also wore a scar in his heart under the medal on his chest. He carried inside the ghosts of the 386 men he believed he had wrongly killed in Vietnam.

Bent on making amends, he became a paramedic. He told his friends he wanted to save 386 lives as penance. The license plate on his car read 386. Although living a seemingly model life for a while, fathering three children with his wife Mary Jo, and serving actively in the local Lutheran Church, Hall's emotional and mental health gradually declined. In 1987, he lost his job. Soon afterwards, he lost his family through a separation. He consumed larger and larger quantities of alcohol and anti-depressant drugs and spent more and more time at the Veteran's Home and Hospital. Doctors diagnosed him as 100 percent disabled because of post-traumatic stress disorder.

The ghosts grew darker. Finally, they destroyed him, their icy fingers pulling him into a final pit of anguish and despair. On September 6, 1990, the Veterans of Post 5555 marched at the funeral for Mike Hall. They had found his body in a motel, dead at thirty-nine, killed by unrevealed causes. Most people said the ghosts finally caught up to him.

His friend Tom Schepers said, "I think what really happened to Hallsy was that body count. Then to have that question raised whether you did the right thing. It was awful for him—and it just got worse." Though Schepers didn't use the word, the implication blares out—guilt stalked Mike Hall and finally pushed him over the ledge to his tragic end.

Whenever we experience guilt, most of us will not descend into the depths that Hall faced.

But, all of us will feel the sharp clutches of guilt's effects to one degree or another. Like an eternal accuser, standing in a never-ending judgment upon our lives, the transgressions we commit rise up in our minds and hearts, a silent sentinel, witnessing to our failures. Guilt's ghosts, whether born of legitimate or illegitimate seed, can affect us in a number of destructive ways.

Lowers Our Self-Esteem

When we transgress our internal moral codes, we find ourselves feeling like failures. We become our own judges—even if no one else judges us harshly—and we conclude we're not particularly valuable to ourselves, to others, or to God. When we own a standard—whether a worthy one or not—and then fall short of it, we cannot help but wonder about our moral strength. We lower our eyes and see our faults dragging at our heels.

Rick Davey, a Hartford, Connecticut, fire investigator, knows the pain that dogs us when we fail. One night in the 1970s he found himself inside a burning house. Charging into a little girl's bedroom, he heard the high-pitched scream of a terrorized child. He saw the closet door that housed the screams. Apparently the child had fled into the closet in desperate search to find a place safe from the fire.

Though blinded by smoke, Davey rushed toward her voice. Tragically, he never reached her. The ceiling over the closet crashed down, and the screaming stopped.

Davey later described his self-recrimination. "I dreamed about her every night for two or three years." As he reported it later, he could see her face clearly in his dreams, "surrounded by flames." His movements toward her were always in slow motion. He awoke many nights in a cold sweat and tortured himself for his failure to save her. "If only I hadn't paused for half a second to hitch up my boots when the fire engine pulled up," he lamented; "if only I had hit the ground running...."

Davey's sense of failure, whether realistic or not, created a guilt that inevitably affected the way he felt about himself. It attacked his self-concept and threatened to burn away his confidence in his ability to serve the public as he should.

The apostle Paul, a man most of us would see as a model of faith and virtue, found himself on more than one occasion fighting this war with low self-esteem. On one occasion he described his inability to live up to the standards of God's grace with this conclusion, "O wretched man that I am! Who will deliver me from this body of death?" (Romans 7:24).

The word "wretched" here refers to one who feels "miserable." The context of these words assures us that Paul feels miserable about himself! He's unable to maintain a Christ-like life because he is "carnal, sold under sin." His self-esteem, the way he views himself in relationship to the world around him, plunges. Certainly, we too find ourselves feeling "wretched" about ourselves when our guilt chips away at the veneer of our self-confidence.

Creates Anger

Whenever we feel an accusing finger pointing at us, from whatever source, we will also experience a certain degree of hostility rising within us. Our hostility could find a target in the one who made us feel the guilt. A teenager curses under his breath at the parent who rightly accuses him of breaking an agreed-upon curfew. A member of the church or synagogue leaves worship angry at the worship leader who reminded him of his duty to support the congregation financially. A businesswoman slams the door on her way out of the office, upset that her boss called her on the carpet for fouling up an important contract. Guilt producers often become anger-receivers.

Not only do we turn our guilt into anger toward others, but we also direct it toward ourselves. We blame ourselves for our failures and generate feelings of self-hatred that we couldn't manage our lives in a better fashion. Obviously, such self-anger, if not handled correctly, can lead to disastrous results. Ultimately, we end up hurting ourselves— either through destructive behaviors like addictions and other hurtful habits, or through the final act of the self-reproachful person—suicide.

We direct our anger at others. We direct it at ourselves. We also direct it at God. When we see we have failed in some way but circumstances leave nothing and no one to blame, we often turn our hostility toward our God.

An ancient tale makes this point well. An old tailor leaves his prayers and walks out of the synagogue. He meets his rabbi on the way out the door. The rabbi asks, "What were you doing in the synagogue, Lev Ashram?"

"I was saying my prayers."

"Good," says the rabbi. "Did you confess your sins?"

"Yes, I confessed my little sins."

"Your little sins?"

"Yes, I confessed that I sometimes cut my cloth on the short side and that I sometimes overcharge my customers just a bit."

"You admitted that to God?"

"Yes, rabbi, I did. I also said 'Lord, I cheat on pieces of cloth. But, you let little babies die. So, I will make you a deal, God. You forgive me my little sins and I will forgive you your big ones.'"

That story makes several points. I hear this one clearly. The rabbi, guilty over his "little sins," deflected his remorse by turning it into anger. He turned his anger toward the God who determined for him the moralities of life. Guilt causes us, at times, to turn in hostility in all directions—toward anyone in our path, even toward our God.

Leads to Depression

In the first chapter I related the tragedy of the suicide of a close friend. I also admitted the guilt that followed as I struggled with whether I had done all I could to prevent Ted's sad end. As I faced the possibility I hadn't sufficiently helped him, I not only faced a lowered sense of self, but I also encountered the dark clouds of a depressed spirit. I found myself questioning whether I could ever do enough. I found myself wondering if my efforts actually helped anyone. My motivation level for ministry dropped as I questioned the value of my meager attempts at ministry.

Depression always follows in the wake of guilt. We tend to think, at least at a subconscious level, that if we feel bad enough, it will pay off the debt owed for our failure. Psychologists place guilt at the head of the class when they identify the wellsprings of depression.

Most of us recognize the name (or at least the face) of Kelly McGillis, star of such blockbuster movies as *Top Gun, Witness,* and *The Accused.* Many of us might not know, however, that in 1978 two men broke into McGillis's

New York apartment and raped her.

As she reported it after the release of *The Accused* (a movie telling the story of a rape victim's search for justice), McGillis suffered from guilt, anger, and depression for years after her tragedy. She said, "For many years I felt as if I had done something wrong.... There will always be a part of me that says I did something to cause that—I must have been a bad girl."

As a result of her sense of guilt, McGillis spent nine unhappy years, depressed about herself and her life. Even her movie success couldn't remove the stain of her discouragement. She fell into alcoholic abuse, and her depression threatened to destroy her life. She reported later, "It wasn't until I started seeing myself self-destructing that I realized I needed help." Fortunately, McGillis found a way out of her depression. Not everyone fares so well.

Harms Our Physical Health

Though it's difficult to determine the extent of physical harm caused to us by guilt, statistics reveal that many of the illnesses of the body actually find their birthplace in an illness of the soul.

We believe we have failed in some way. We didn't call our parents for several weeks. We cheated on a test. We messed up a major contract. We spent more money than we should have on clothes. We missed our nine-year-old girl's baseball game. Over time guilt builds up. It eats away at our insides. It causes an ulcer. It sends us to a doctor. The doctor puts us in the hospital for tests. He prescribes a change in our diet and sends us to a pharmacist for an antacid. He advises us to reduce our stress level. The doctor has treated a symptom. The guilt created the health problem, but the doctor can write no prescription for our guilt.

Who can deny that our guilt weighs us down, drives us into stress-related disorders, causes heart problems, pushes up our blood pressure and makes us prone to accidents? A person with a healthy guilt is a person with an unhealthy body.

Leads to Paralysis of Action

Recently, on a trip to Nashville, Tennessee, I found myself waiting for a late-arriving airplane flight. Frustrated at the delay, I stood at the window with my arms crossed and impatiently peered out at the departing and landing planes. I watched a 747 jet taxi to the terminal. As it stopped, a blue-uniformed worker scurried toward it. The worker shoved a triangular-shaped black object under its wheels. Then, he walked away to other duties.

That picture stuck in my mind. A tiny block of wood placed strategically under the wheels of that huge plane kept it from moving. That "chock" kept that plane stuck in place.

Guilt serves as a "chock" in many lives, keeping us from moving ahead because we're devastated by our failures of the past. We wonder if anything we do now or in the future can ever succeed.

In the New Testament we discover a fascinating encounter between Jesus and a paralytic man brought to him for healing. Instead of immediately dealing with the physical ailment that prevented the lame man from walking, Jesus ministered to his spiritual and emotional circumstances. He said to the paralyzed man, "Son, your sins are forgiven you." Immediately the man "arose, took up the bed, and went out in the presence of them all" (Mark 2: 1-12).

Though we cannot know exactly what motivatẽd Jesus to respond this way, we can say he recognized a truth most psychologists accept and common sense reveals. Our "sin" and the guilt that results from it often places us on the bed of emotional, spiritual, and even physical paralysis.

We label people who can't react to the stimuli of life "catatonic." Though this word is a clinical term for people who don't respond physically, I think we can also use it to describe people so tied to the stakes of guilt that they cannot get on with life. These tragic people allow their woundedness to drive them into an emotional cave. They refuse to move, shut off from the stimuli of the outside world. Transfixed, they sit and stare, unable to step out of their darkness.

Though most of us don't succumb to these sad depths, we can reach the point of feeling unable to move ahead and reach any solution to our problems. Guilt slams the door to action, and we know no way to unlock it. So long as our "sin" remains lodged in our minds and hearts, we will continue in our lethargy.

Not too many years ago, a church member asked me to visit a family member who wouldn't come out of his bedroom. As the concerned lady said, "He's stuck there." I followed up on the request and discovered an apparently normal man in his mid-thirties who had gradually declined in his emotional health. It had started six months prior to my visit when his employer of fifteen years had fired him. After receiving his pink slip, he had searched for work for about two weeks. Then, he stopped trying and stayed home. Next, he refused to leave his front yard. Then, he wouldn't step outside his home. When I arrived, he wouldn't go out of his bedroom.

As we talked, he laughed at his predicament. "I guess I'll be in the closet next." His humor, however, was short-lived as he concluded, "I'm afraid to go out since I lost my job. If I get another job, I'm afraid I'm such a screw-up I'll just lose it too." Guilt tied him with strings of fear to a tiny room and prevented him from acting in a reasonable way. It can do the same to us.

Wayne Dyer, a popular speaker, author, and psychologist, summed up the paralyzing nature of guilt. He said, "Guilt means that you use up your present moments being immobilized.... With guilt you focus on a past event, feel dejected or angry about something you did or said, and use up your present moments being occupied with feelings over past behavior."

Leads to a Drive Toward Good Works

On the opposite end of the room from the catatonic people whose guilt freezes them into inactivity, stand those whose guilt propels them to a frenzy of activity in an effort to make up for past transgressions. These people somehow feel that if they can do enough, they can pay off their debt and absolve their guilt. The former reprobate gets reformed and automatically changes into a zealous proponent of hyper-morality and energetic spirituality. Like a geyser spewing forth steam from an underground source of heat and water, these people pour out the white-hot guilt that has bubbled in them through a combination of good works and high powered intentions.

We can't always know if the person responding in this way has genuinely reformed. Often they have. Sometimes, though, it seems their "reformation" has ulterior motives.

In April of 1992, Leona Helmsley, the millionaire "Hotel Queen" went to prison for income tax evasion. Known for her lavish and arrogant life-style prior to her arrest and trial, Mrs. Helmsley suddenly experienced a change of heart. She offered to open her glitzy hotels to the homeless if the authorities wouldn't send her to prison. No one bought it. She went to jail. Guilt can propel us to genuine good works or to manipulative efforts in hopes we can restore ourselves to the good graces of our friends or our God.

Leads to Isolation

In an old story, an elderly couple putters down the highway one Sunday afternoon in their well-maintained 1952 Studebaker. The man hunches over the steering wheel while his gray-haired wife sits securely wedged against the passenger door.

Suddenly, a car swooshes by them. The aged lady, noting the young man and woman squeezed together like Siamese twins in the front seat of the passing car, complains to her husband, "You know, Wilbur, we used to sit like that." Wilbur nods as he looks knowingly across the vast expanse of seat at his wife. He concludes, "Yeah, we did....But you know what? In all these years, I haven't moved an inch!"

Somehow, over the years, the dear wife had gradually edged her way further and further from her husband. Now, a gulf of car seat separated them. That story illustrates what often happens as we allow guilt to pile up in our lives. Guilt creates a sense of separation between persons.

We see this in everyday life. A husband drinks too much and his drunkenness drives him into a verbal tirade against his wife. When he sobers up, he desperately desires forgiveness. But, he's so guilt-stricken he refuses to look his wife in the eye, much less reach out to her for help.

A teenager refuses to study. Poor grades keep her from attending college. Her parents, who encourage and support her, want to assure her of their acceptance in spite of her failure. But, the youth cannot believe that her parents won't say, "I told you so." Besides, she realizes that if they do, they have every right. Instead of receiving her parent's help, the girl rebels and pushes them further away.

How often in circumstances too numerous to illustrate, have we heard people lament, "I can never face that person again. I've fouled up so royally, I can't bear to see the one I've disappointed."

Inevitably, this attitude also invades our spiritual relationship with our God. Time and time again, I have watched believers fall away from the spiritual relationship of their faith as a direct result of a perceived transgression. They cannot or will not forgive themselves and don't believe anyone else will either. They wear their guilt like a scarlet **G** on their hearts and believe that they cannot approach God because of their mistake. They avoid the places of contact with God—the sanctuary of worship, the closet of prayer, and the pages of Scripture because these cause the **G** to beam out like a neon light in Las Vegas. Instead of turning to God for forgiveness and restoration, they flee from God and hide out in spiritual isolation. The scriptural account of human beginnings depicts this for us in graphic terminology.

Adam and Eve, our spiritual parents, transgressed the established will of God as they ate from the tree of the knowledge of good and evil in the middle of the Garden. This transgression created an immediate awareness in them, and they recognized their "nakedness." Although Genesis doesn't elaborate on the meaning of this, it tells us that they quickly made clothes for themselves, covering up from each other. Then, significantly, when God approached them, "they hid from the Lord God among the trees of the garden." And God called out, "Where are you?"

These spiritual ancestors of ours acted out our present responses. They ran from the presence of God. Their guilt spurred them as they wrapped the leaves around their waists and hunkered down under the bushes. The plaintive words of God and the actions of Adam and Eve show us the eternal results of our failures. They create distance between us as we cover up from each other and hide behind the trees, staying out of the sight of God.

Leads to Self-Destruction

Ultimately, we hear this message from the tragic end of Mike Hall: Guilt can eat away at the walls of our personal selves so completely that it eventually destroys us. It doesn't always consume us to the point we commit physical suicide, but it certainly has that potential.

Christopher Allison, in his work *Guilt, Anger and God,* put it this way: "We resolve our guilt by little deaths of withdrawal from life and by the hope of self-damaging behavior. It is not just the compulsive gambler, the alcoholic, or the neurotically accident-prone personality who are the victims of self-damage. All of us, to some extent, . . . get involved in patterns that are drastically self-damaging and even threaten our existence."

Anyone even vaguely familiar with the story of Jesus knows the name of Judas. Known as "The Betrayer" for his deed of treachery toward the Nazarene, Judas made the mistake of trying to control what Jesus did. He turned Jesus over to the authorities in the effort to force Jesus to reveal himself as the long-awaited military messiah of the Jews. Sadly for Judas, Jesus refused that manner of leadership and accepted death on the crucifix.

We don't know what Judas did on the long night following the arrest of Jesus. As the elders of Jerusalem deliberated Jesus' fate, I suspect he waited at a distance. I suspect he hoped and prayed that Jesus would erupt in a divine fury, fling Himself at His accusers and prove his lordship to the nations of Israel and Rome. Yet, that didn't happen. The night passed.

The next morning the sunshine snaked into

his room and Judas awoke from his troubled sleep. Frantically recalling the night's events, Judas rushed to the temple to get the news. "What?" he asked the Roman guards. "They've condemned Jesus to death?...No! They couldn't do that!" But they had.

I can see Judas holding his hands up to his face, inspecting them, seeing the blood of Jesus on them. He tries to rub it off, but can't. The stain clings to his skin. He runs to his home and picks up the sack of silver coins the priests had paid him for his treachery. Clutching his blood bounty, he sprints to the temple. He would return the money! That would atone for his sin. The money wasn't important anyway. Crashing into the presence of the priests, Judas flings the silver onto the table. "Here. I don't want this. Let him go. He's not a threat to you."

The priests and elders laugh. "So! Your conscience is bothering you. That means nothing to us. Take care of it yourself." Judas retreats from the room and descends into his own private hell. He watches the crucifixion from a distance, cursing himself for his sin, yet hoping that Jesus will rip himself off the cross in a last minute blaze of righteous glory. It doesn't happen.

Judas's heart plummets as the soldiers lower the body of Jesus from the cross and transport it to the tomb of Joseph. The turmoil surging inside him reaches its crest. "Why did you betray Jesus?" he interrogates himself. "A tragic mistake. Now he's dead, at your hands!"

Reeling from his deed, Judas pulls a rope from his satchel, staggers to a nearby tree and chokes out his own life. Though listed in Scripture as a suicide, Judas's death was actually a murder. The bony fingers of guilt placed the noose around his neck and squeezed the life out of a repentant man.

Although no one can know for sure, I suspect that guilt has murdered millions throughout the centuries of human experience. Uncaught, it will continue to stalk its victims— people like Judas, like Mike Hall, like your friends and family members, like yourself— pushing and prodding them to walk the path which crashes over the abyss of self-destruction.

V

Empty at the Center

The Value of Legitimate Guilt

Kenneth Bianchi fooled everyone. He wore phony police badges to fool his victims. He worked for a while as a uniformed security guard. He once owned and operated a false counseling service, dispensing advice to others to help with their personal problems.

Then, in 1977, this man who appeared so normal, kidnapped, raped, tortured, and murdered ten Los Angeles girls and women between the ages of twelve and twenty-eight. The media dubbed him the Hillside Strangler because he dumped his victims on a hill near the city.

Thankfully, the police finally captured Bianchi, and the reign of terror ceased. Later at the trial that followed Bianchi's arrest, the judge, shocked by the heinous acts of violence,

79

said Bianchi was "incapable of feeling remorse."

In the preceding chapter, we looked at the potentially harmful effects of guilt. Given its destructive potential, we're tempted to say guilt has absolutely no value for our lives. We're tempted to declare guilt a totally illegitimate child in our family of emotional reactions.

Many "pop" authors and trained psychologists have seemingly yielded to this temptation. Without distinguishing between genuine and false remorse, these people speak of guilt as an evil we should exorcise from our lives like a demon. Seeing only the negative side of guilt, these writers and thinkers see it as a barrier to the promised land of joy and fulfillment.

Robert Anthony, a noted psychologist and author, leads the parade of those who want to deny any value to guilt. "Guilt is totally unnecessary and self-destructive."

In his book *Your Erroneous Zones,* popular speaker Wayne Dyer calls guilt a "futile emotion" and adds that it is the "most useless of all erroneous zone behaviors. It is by far the greatest waste of emotional energy." Dyer suggests that guilt should be "exterminated, spray-cleaned and sterilized forever" from our lives.

Unless I'm misreading the plain language of these writers, they're saying guilt has *absolutely no value* for the person who wants to fully appreciate and enjoy life. They see guilt only as a hindrance to happiness.

Though I concur that guilt can lead potentially to destructive behavior, I cannot agree with those who say all guilt *necessarily* causes negative responses.

The realization that guilt *can* sometimes lead to painful behavior should not lead us to the false assumption that guilt *always* hurts us. Though we tend to assume all guilt harms us, people like Ken Bianchi remind us that remorse serves a valuable function within the human personality and the human community. Without guilt as a spiritual and emotional restraint, we would find ourselves engulfed by the savagery that potentially lies within each of us.

We see such savagery loosened most graphically in the life of Charles Manson, one of America's most notorious murderers. Speaking of the night of his infamous rampage of death, Manson later said, "I was aware of being totally without conscience." What a chilling possibility—that we might live without any sense of conscience and the guilt that arises from it!

Without guilt as a harness, most of us probably wouldn't succumb to a Manson-type evil.
We, however, would certainly find ourselves
acting in ways we don't normally find acceptable. A husband or wife could commit adultery
and feel no pricks of conscience. Corporate
leaders could steal from the shareholders, and
no one would feel any drive to blow the
whistle. Insiders on Wall Street could manipulate the market to the detriment of the
American people, and no one would care. We
could lie, kill, cheat, and hate and never experience a struggle within the soul because of our
actions. Though a few might find this attractive
for themselves, they certainly wouldn't want
the other person not to have a conscience!
Which one of us can deny that guilt serves a
valuable purpose in human society? Society
cannot exist without the constraints of an
internal code of action to govern its people. We
rightly fear the person who feels no guilt for
that person has fallen to the depths of the beast
and sees other people as prey.

Psychologists call the condition of living
without a conscience, an "anti personality disorder." In this condition, people act without
regard to "normal" patterns of thought.

Unfortunately, such persons often disguise themselves so well with a facade of normalcy that society doesn't easily recognize them. These conscience-deficient people live and work in every strata of society and business. They have power and influence, often serving as business leaders and political officials.

People of this type, says the universally acclaimed psychologist and author Scott Peck, are not "crazy as ordinarily perceived. Instead, they deny the suffering of their guilt.... by casting pain onto others .... They cause suffering. They create a sick society.

We cannot know for certain what happens to destroy the inner codes of conduct that usually prohibit such misfortunate actions. I have two theories. First, it's possible that some people are born with no conscience. Through a physiological malfunction, their genetic make-up includes no "morality DNA." Like blank sheets of paper, these rare individuals step into the world with no innate knowledge of right and wrong and never attain this knowledge through their experiences. Neither society, nor parent, nor religion can penetrate their inner void to fill it with the cloak of morality. They exist like a transparency, too slick for any code of conduct to stick.

Second, it's possible that once present in the individual, the conscience disappears, is covered over by circumstances of the environment, callused by abuse and the rough edges of life's pains. This tragic individual, faced with coping with the harshness of life, begins to ignore the inner voice. Striving to survive the sharp stings of childhood and maturity, the shrill voice of the conscience grows dimmer and dimmer, finally ceasing to be heard at all.

The ancestors of modern Native Americans believed the conscience was a three-cornered stone lodged in the bosom. Each time the individual violated the conscience, the stone turned over and the violator felt the sharp cut of it. With each successive transgression and each subsequent turn, however, the sharp edges of the stone wore off a little, even as it cut and made its presence known. Gradually, over time, as the person continually broke the inner code, they rounded off the corners of the stone until it no longer cut as it should. Thus, the conscience disappeared as an agent of inner conviction.

No matter the reason for the lack of conscience, we do know some people who *seem* to live without guilt. We know such persons exist in every level of society. We know they cause immense personal and corporate pain. That knowledge causes us to admit the value of legitimate guilt. I suspect most of the aversion to accepting guilt as a reasonable response stems from the reality that far too many of us suffer from a "neurotic" guilt. I've called this an "illegitimate" guilt because it stems from inappropriate sources.

Illegitimate guilt, born of situations beyond our control, never serves a useful function. We *should* exterminate it from our lives at the earliest opportunity. The destructiveness of the inappropriate guilt should not, though, also destroy the potential value of legitimate remorse.

Thankfully, a majority of both religious theologians and secular psychologists agree with my conclusions and admit to the necessity of some sense of guilt. Leslie Weatherhead, a world-renowned writer early in the twentieth century said it well: "It would be absurd to suppose that any sense of guilt in the mind of a person indicated an abnormality which ought to be removed. Normal guilt I equate with the theological 'sense of sin' which ought to follow the doing of wrong."

Legitimate guilt, if handled correctly, acts as a helpful "transition emotion" for us. By that, I mean it serves as a bridge between two shores of life. It carries us from an action, thought, or response that our conscience deems inappropriate, unacceptable, or sinful to a place of confession, restoration, and forgiveness. Guilt provides us an opportunity to learn and mature as we resolve our inner qualms and find peace with ourselves again. We should not get stuck in guilt, but neither should we try to ignore it and leap over it.

Let me offer an illustration of the way guilt should act. Less than ten miles from my home in Jefferson City, Missouri, the snake-like curves of the Missouri River wind their way toward the Mississippi. To cross this muddy gulf, the state of Missouri has constructed a number of bridges at key points. A month ago workers completed the construction of a new bridge across Highway 54 to allow faster and easier access to travelers through the heart of the state.

When we look at any bridge, we'll see two shores or landing points and we'll see people at various places in their crossings. Some will already be on the far side; others will stand somewhere in route. A third group will just be getting started on the passage. The bridge serves as the connecting point over which people pass. People can't leap to the other shore without the assistance of a bridge. The bridge acts as a necessary go-between from one shore to the other.

Guilt can serve us in a similar fashion—as a bridge, as a transition ground from the transgressions of our past, to the remorse of the present, to the resolution of the future. When that occurs, it moves us ahead in two positive ways.

A Problem Indicator

I know almost nothing about auto mechanics. In fact, other than putting in the gas and starting the ignition, I do nothing else to maintain my car. Fortunately for me, and for millions of others in my situation, my car came with a built in "indicator light" that tells me when something goes wrong. When the engine needs attention, a light illuminates on my dashboard. It tells me, "Check Engine." Guilt should function the same way. It acts as a blinking light on the panel of our lives warning us to check our systems.

When the light flashes on my instrument panel, I then decide whether or not to take the car to a mechanic to get it checked. Typically, I head to the garage. And, usually, the light indicates the need for a tune-up on my car.

On at least one recent visit, though, the mechanic told me, "I can't find anything wrong with your engine, but your *check engine* light has a short in it and comes on when it shouldn't!"

When we have a problem in our lives because of a wrong committed (as we understand wrong and right), the light of guilt will flash into our consciousness. Certainly, our perceptions of right and wrong may be skewed (the light might need fixing instead of the engine) and we might need to correct that perception. Guilt, though, acts to protect us in those occasions when our perception blinks clearly and when we have actually transgressed a reasonable code of conduct or thought.

When the light goes off, we find ourselves responding—either to ignore it and run into trouble later or to check it and see if a real problem exists. When guilt performs that task, it has served us well.

A Change Motivator

As the light reminding us of a potential problem, guilt causes us to consider making necessary changes to keep the "engine" running well. If a problem in our actions exist, guilt prods us to fix it. The guilt continues to disturb us on the inside, to rumble around in our minds and hearts until we take some step to either alleviate it or cover it over. The painful aspects of guilt encourage us to make it right, to cease the action or thought that lights up the panel of our conscience. *It coaxes us to change unacceptable behavior.*

Not too long ago, I visited with a young man who had recently checked himself into an alcohol rehabilitation program. He hoped the program could help him get control of his addiction. The center treated him immediately with the drug Anabuse. This drug causes a sick stomach and vomiting if the person actually ingests alcohol. The doctors hope the person taking it will detest the sickness it creates, will associate the drug with the sickness, and will refrain from drinking.

That analogy shows how guilt often works. Guilt *is* a negative feeling. We don't like to experience it. Yet, as we've seen, we wouldn't want to exist as a person without a conscience. So, the negative feeling serves a positive purpose! We need guilt. Like the pain we feel when we place our hand on a hot stove burner, guilt warns us to move away from what hurts us or others. It acts as an "aversion" technique, turning us away from what harms us.

Not only does guilt encourage us to cease unacceptable behavior, but it also *encourages us to embrace positive behavior.* At the same time that guilt turns us away from the hurtful, it also steers us toward the helpful. It points us toward a way of response that will bring peace and harmony to us.

James Dobson, a much-read author and much-heard speaker, once said, "Personal disapproval for wrong behavior is absolutely essential if change for the better is to occur." When we bump against our conscience (with our real or perceived infractions against it), we create a troubling disharmony within ourselves. Naturally, we seek a way of quieting this inner distress. Often, we end the unrest only when we choose a right way over a wrong way to live.

The name Charles Colson rings a bell in the minds of most of us today. Since 1975 he has made himself familiar because of his untiring efforts to carry the message of faith into the prison systems of our nation. Going where so many of us hesitate to walk, Colson, through his Prison Fellowship, dares to enter the jungles of crime and depravity. Surrounded by tough-bitten guards, speaking to the dregs of our society, Colson obviously believes in the God of whom he speaks.

It has not always been this way, however. For those who may not know, Colson the prison minister, was once better known as Colson, the Hatchet Man for the Richard Nixon administration. As the *Wall Street Journal* reported in a story in October of 1975, "Colson would walk over his own grandmother if he had to."

At that point in life, Colson cared for nothing else but power. He craved it and he gave his soul for it. It became the consuming passion of his life, to the point he closed his eyes to the ethical implications of his actions and to the potential hurt to himself, to his family, and to his nation.

As history reminds us, the Nixon administration ran afoul of the moral conscience of a disappointed nation. As the presidency collapsed around him, Colson discovered that his cherished but misguided values also sank underneath him. He began to despair of life itself. He began to feel the pangs of conscience gnawing at his insides.

At this point Colson began to consider Christian faith. Through the fiasco of Watergate and during the season of his life when all seemed to fail, Colson slowly came to the point of belief. Finally, after months of searching, he recognized his drive for power had brought not joy, but jadedness and guilt. Colson made a decision. He would believe. He would trust God.

Sitting one morning beside the ocean he loved, Colson accepted the reality of Jesus Christ. At that point, he writes, "came a sureness of mind that matched the depth of feeling in my heart. There came something more: strength and serenity, a wonderful new assurance about life, a fresh perception of myself and the world around me. In the process, I felt old fears, tensions, and animosities draining away. I was coming alive to things I'd never seen before; as if God was filling the barren void I'd known for so many months, filling it to its brim with a whole new kind of awareness."

Colson experienced change. He embraced a new way of life. His conscience drove him to it. His guilt moved him to a point of transformation. Now, even the cynics admit, Colson provides caring ministry for the prisoners of our society.

Anyone who has ever watched the waves of the ocean crashing against a retaining wall knows how this happens. The weighty force of the tide slams the wall of water ashore. But when the water hits the retaining wall, it backs up against itself and churns up the seas. Instead of a gentle wash onto the beach, the wave turns into a dangerous whirlpool.

The retaining wall of our internal morality refuses to allow our transgressions to crash unimpeded into our lives. Instead, it knocks them backward, creating the disharmony of our guilt, swirling about in our spirits, looking for a way to move to quieter waters. The white foam of guilt drives us to search for a place of harmony and peace. It drives us to make changes for the better, to put away old patterns and accept new possibilities. Before we can accept these new possibilities, though, we need to make clear the distinction between genuine and false remorse.

VI

A Shot in the Leg

Identifying False Guilt

The three friends trudged single file back to the main road, weary from a tough day hunting quail in the fields outside of Cleburne, Texas. Their dogs, with tongues lolling over their teeth from exertion, pranced in and out of their masters' steps, proud of their catch. The men, too tired to talk much, headed up a muddy path, anxious to reach their horse-drawn carriage. One of the men, tired of the weight of the gun on one shoulder, shifted it to the other. Unexpectedly, the crack of the gun ricocheted through the gray sky and Captain J. C. Arnold, a member of the Texas Rangers and Police Chief of Dallas, Texas, staggered and fell—the victim of a shotgun full of birdshot in the leg.

Immediately, Arnold's friends rushed the captain back to Dallas and into the hospital.

The doctors assured them the leg wound wasn't serious. Tragically though, Arnold died from an unrelated coronary thrombosis within two days.

All eyes now turned to the man who had accidentally shot the Captain. His name was George W. Truett; he served as the pastor of the First Baptist Church of Dallas. The doctors told Truett the Captain's death wasn't the result of the gunshot wounds. He would have died anyway.

The words of the doctors didn't console him. He fell into a deep depression. Though he accepted the accidental nature of the tragedy, he couldn't excuse himself for what he saw as his carelessness. He believed he had killed one of his best friends. He castigated himself, thinking the "blood of a friend" would forever stain his hands. Truett concluded he could never preach again—that he would leave the ministry. He went into seclusion.

The people of Dallas rallied to encourage him. From Wednesday, the night Arnold died, until Saturday evening, scores of letters and well-wishers contacted Truett, reminding him of their concern and asserting again and again the accidental nature of the misfortune. He hid himself at home, reading the Bible, trying to come to grips with the emotions surging through him, threatening to drown him.

Saturday night Truett dreamed. In his dream, the Lord Jesus appeared. Truett awoke, then fell asleep again. The dream repeated itself two more times. In each instance, Jesus repeated the words: "Be not afraid. You are My man from now on."

Upon awaking the next morning, Truett decided he had to preach in spite of his guilt. He entered the pulpit and shared his heart. But, his preaching changed from that point. For the remainder of his life Truett's preaching was marked by a compassion and an urgency not experienced until this. His attitude shifted and he became known in legend as the preacher who never smiled.

Throughout these pages, I've spoken of two kinds of guilt. One, which I've called "legitimate," potentially serves a valuable purpose as it spurs us ahead to repentance, forgiveness, and reconciliation. The second type, the one I've called "illegitimate" guilt, serves no positive purpose at all. It hurts us, it keep us in chains of remorse, it blocks personal growth.

Most of us would agree that Truett labored

under an illegitimate guilt—a remorse from a death that he didn't cause and couldn't prevent. But, that made his pain no less real. Certainly, guilt *feels* the same whether it's legitimate or not. The queasy feeling that grabs the pit of the stomach, the migraine headache that ties a knot around the skull, or the lead barbells that press down on the shoulders don't discriminate between "types" of guilt as they do their dirty work on our emotions and spirits.

Yet, though the feeling remains equal, the validity of the source of the struggle is not. After all, a person can suffer similar pain caused by different diseases. Recently, I've heard two people describe their headache pain in precisely identical words. "It feels like my head's in a vise and somebody is squeezing it."

The feeling was the same. But, the diagnosis diverged completely. X-rays revealed a brain tumor in one of the patients. The doctor diagnosed poor vision in the other. The different sources of an identical pain led the respective doctors to prescribe divergent treatments for the two ailments.

We should follow a similar pattern as we seek to deal with our guilt. We begin by diagnosing our guilts. We refuse to make the mistake of lumping all our guilt together and treating it the with one prescription. We recognize we can't alleviate all guilt with the same methods.

We find ourselves, therefore, facing the question: "How can we know whether the guilt we feel is illegitimate or legitimate?" If we're going to find a method to deal effectively with our remorse, we must first scrutinize our guilts and place them in the correct camp. To help us do that, I want to consider five illegitimate causes of guilt.

Guilt Caused by Unbidden Thoughts

Have you ever found yourself watching the movements of an attractive member of the opposite sex walking past you on the beach? Have you ever felt an anger rise in your throat as an inconsiderate driver cut you off in freeway traffic? Have you ever sensed a surge of jealousy overpower you momentarily when you heard that a co-worker received the promotion you hoped to get? I suspect you could answer yes to all three of these examples. Amazingly, these examples don't express at all the more destructive ideas that sometimes push out of our inner selves. Any thought, no matter how obscene, harmful, or criminal, can overcome us momentarily. Thoughts and emotions arise within us so quickly that we often feel unable to stifle them. If our internal codes tell us we shouldn't feel this way toward these people, we will find guilt arising almost simultaneously with the unbidden thoughts.

Obviously, we should not dwell on these thoughts as they punch their way out of our subconscious into our conscious minds. But, neither can we reasonably expect ourselves to live without such images. As Martin Luther, the father of the Protestant Reformation, said it, "We cannot prevent the birds from flying over our heads, but we can prevent them from building nests in our hair."

A guilt created by a "bird flying over our heads" or an unbidden thought flitting through our heads lives as an illegitimate guilt.

Guilt Created by Uncontrollable Forces

On September 22, 1989, Hurricane Hugo, one of the most destructive and costly natural disaster ever to strike the United States, swept furiously ashore on the South Carolina coast.

After devastating the Charleston area, it plowed inland, chewing up trees, spitting out houses, and crunching everything in its path. Just after midnight, Hugo's full anger punched into Sumter, South Carolina.

Stretched out on her sofa in her den (the room with the fewest windows), Mrs. Venetta Rogers, seventy-six and almost blind, anxiously listened to the sounds outside. She heard the wind rip trees from the ground and toss them against the side of the condominium duplex where she lived. She heard rain crackling down, sounding like small arms gunfire as it peppered her windows.

With the power out, the telephone silent, and the batteries in her radio dead, she had no way to get news. Unsuccessfully, she tried to sleep. By candlelight she looked at her watch—almost two A.M. How much longer could this horror last? The wind seemed to pick up its pace—growling now, like a wounded lion, pacing with frenzy outside her walls trying to get in at her.

Suddenly, her roof opened! A wet and ponderous shadow crashed down toward her. With a speed created by fear, she jerked her frail body off the sofa and dove into the corner of the room, barely dodging the five-feet thick, fifty-feet-tall pine tree that split her condominium den in half as it thundered to the floor.

Exposed to the elements now, Mrs. Rogers wondered, "Should I stay put and try to ride out the storm? Or will another tree crash down on me? Should I try to make it next door?" She hoped the Wilson family was home. She made her decision.

Grimly determined, she stood up and picked her way to the door. She leaned her 115-pound body into the wind, holding her sweater to her chest. She sprinted unsteadily the thirty yards that separated her place from her neighbors. Miraculously, she made it. Drenched and pale, she knocked. Her neighbors heard her. They opened the door and let her in. She rode out the storm with them. Though placed in the hospital for two days afterwards for minor cuts and abrasions, Venetta survived.

Two days later her son visited me and poured out his grief. His mom had called him the day before Hugo and had pleaded with him to come stay with her that night. Unfortunately, he had business plans out of town and he refused to change them. Reminding her of the weather reports at the time, he had said:

"Mom, by the time hurricanes make it this far inland they've lost most of their power. The weather report says we won't get much more than fifty-to-sixty mile-an-hour winds. You'll be fine."

The weather reports had steered him wrong, and now guilt crushed down on him. "I'll never forgive myself. What if she had died?"

As we talked, it dawned on me, guilt tormented this son not because he was uncaring or inattentive to his mom. Instead, it gripped him because he had been unable to foresee certain natural events. Unable to control the forces of a violent storm, he now castigated himself for it.

I've watched this happen in a variety of other settings. A parent allows a teenager to use the car for the first time, and a drunken driver plows into the youth on that same night, causing paralysis. The parents blame themselves for the tragedy.

A businessman with two college-aged children expands in the height of an economic boom. Suddenly, the economy goes bust, and the business crashes, he has no money for tuition, and his kids stay home that fall. The man points the finger at himself for not foreseeing the recession. In a thousand dramatic and not so dramatic ways, we beat ourselves up for circumstances completely out of our control. That's an illegitimate guilt which has no seat at the table of genuine reasons for remorse.

I like the way Nathaniel Branden said it in his best-selling work, *Honoring the Self:* "Where there is no power, there can be no responsibility, and where there is no responsibility, there can be no reasonable self-reproach. Regret yes; guilt no."

Guilt Caused by Another's Failures

I'll never forget the stare on Robert's face as he walked out of the courtroom. Convicted for the third time for possessing cocaine and passing bad checks, Robert had been sentenced to four years in prison. Tragically, Robert refused to accept responsibility for his actions and continued to place the blame on others for his mistakes. As the police officers escorted him out of the room, he stopped for a second to speak to his wife. He hissed the words: "If it weren't for you, I wouldn't be here in this mess. If you supported me like a good wife should, I wouldn't have turned out this way."

Although that woman moved from our community soon afterward and I never had the opportunity to talk with her about her feelings, I can well imagine the anguish her husband's words surely stirred up in her. He "guilted" her by blaming her for his personal failures.

Most of us are familiar with the Genesis account of the first transgression of the human race. Because we've heard it often, we tend to overlook much of its message for us. When Adam blamed Eve, saying to God, "The woman you gave to me, gave me the fruit of the tree, and I did eat," we automatically shake our heads at his attempts to pass off his faults onto another. Typically, while we're castigating Adam for his failure to accept his responsibility, we fail to consider the effect this had on our primordial mother. Though the writers of Genesis don't look at the events of the Fall through the eyes of the woman, they would perhaps not mind if we did.

Wouldn't this attempt to blame her cause a "guilt trip," to enter her spirit? And, wrongfully so? Wouldn't she possibly wonder as God cast them both out of the Garden, "Was this all my fault?" Unfortunately, one person can "guilt" another through an inappropriate accusation.

The primary message of the Fall is that we

all face the responsibility of choice. Though each one reacted in a chain of events, each one embraced the temptation individually. That's why the writers detailed the sequence so carefully. The woman ate, then the man. Both made their own individual choices. Neither had the right to blame the other. Yet, automatically, each one did.

We still do. And, when we do, we inevitably create guilt, even if undeserved, in the person on whom we dump the garbage of our excuses. This happens in dramatic and in mundane circumstances.

An elderly mother calls a daughter and says, "If you would come see me more often, I wouldn't get so depressed." A child says to a parent, "If you let me have a little more freedom, I wouldn't be so rebellious." A husband says to a wife, "If you would exercise with me, I could lose some of this weight." A boss says to her employees, "If all of you had worked harder, we could have had better profits this year."

Whenever someone else blames a failure of theirs on you and you feel guilt nipping at your heels, pause and ask yourself this question: "Am I genuinely responsible for what happened to them?" If the answer is no, then reject that illegitimate guilt.

Guilt Caused by Accepting Another's Moralities

Whether we consciously recognize it or not, the moralities accepted by some people don't always deserve adherence by everyone else. Not too long ago, a friend of mine went to Germany to work with Christians for two weeks in Christian missions. The German Christians, primarily West Germans, were trying to share their beliefs with thousands of former East Germans who had heard almost nothing of Christian faith since World War II. During his visit, my friend Ed witnessed scores of German Christians enjoying their nightly mugs of beer. What an eye-opener for a good Baptist from Georgia!

As he described to me, "The Georgia Baptists couldn't understand how the German Christians could drink beer, and the German Christians in turn couldn't understand how American Christian women could wear so much make-up."

This experience, which seems quaint to many of us, teaches one valuable lesson—what serves as a morality for one need not necessarily serve as a morality for another. We all grew up with family, regional, and national moralities placed on us.

I remember an interview I once had with an East Texas Baptist church as it sought a youth minister. A blue-haired woman asked me, "What do you think of mixed bathing?"

Trying to bring some humor to the situation, I answered, "I think everyone ought to shower alone."

She didn't laugh. She meant, "What did I think about boys and girls swimming together?" I saw no problem with it, but this Texas church did. Even in 1980.

Needless to say, I didn't get the job. But, I did get the point! People will place their moralities on us unless we're careful to test them for their validity. Parents do this as they phrase issues of safety, convenience, or efficiency in moral terms. We get labeled "bad" if we run across the street without holding a parent's hand; if we dye our hair purple; if a guy wears an earring.

When anyone makes matters of taste, personal style, or individual preference a question of moral theology, we're tempted to accept it for ourselves. That creates illegitimate guilt in us.

Your immediate supervisor works until 7:00 each night, and takes work home even then. He glowers at you when you leave at 5:30 without a briefcase full of papers. You can't enjoy your normal fifty-hour workweek because he works sixty-five and makes you feel guilty that you don't.

If you discover your guilt arises because another person seeks to impose their standards on you, make sure their morality has a basis other than their own culture and context. Otherwise, you may be feeling an illegitimate guilt.

Guilt Caused by Amoral Failures

Not too long ago I watched the conclusion of a Big Eight college basketball game on television. As the game wound down to the end, the two teams were tied with three seconds to go. A freshman guard stood on the free throw line with two attempts to score. Sadly for him and his team, he missed both shots, and his team eventually lost in overtime.

Afterward, a sports reporter interviewed the

freshman as he walked off the court. With his head dragging his chest, the despondent youngster moaned, "I feel so bad. I lost this game. I let my team down."

Thankfully, the announcer showed a little sensitivity and didn't prolong the interview. The image of that eighteen-year-old player stayed with me long after I switched off the set. His face showed his feelings. He felt "bad" as he said, guilty that he had failed himself and his team.

Often we find ourselves facing circumstances in which we don't succeed, in spite of our best efforts. Then, when we fail, we tend to place the ball and chain of guilt around our ankles and wear it far past the actual failure itself. Typically, we do this in spite of the fact that our failures occur in circumstances that have nothing to do with genuine morality. We feel like we've done something bad (or at least that we've not done something good) even though the matter has no connection to a moral choice of right and wrong.

A father working desperately to make financial ends meet so he can send his child to college finds that his best efforts don't generate enough income to achieve his goal; the bitter bile of guilt rises up in his stomach. A third-grader studies hard for all "A's" to make her parents happy, but ends up with one "B plus." She cries when she hands them her report card. A doctor's patient dies on the operating table during heart surgery. A high school debater forgets the point during the response, and the team loses.

In each of these situations, guilt chews away on the person in spite of the reality that none of these are moral issues. They are expectation issues. We may expect perfection, but we will not achieve it. Yet, our unrealistic expectations of constant success create such a standard within us that anything short of that gives birth to guilt.

As you consider your feelings of failure and the guilt that so often accompanies them, ask yourself: "Did I make my best effort? Is my failure a morality issue? Is it an expectation issue?" Knowing the difference between moral and amoral issues can help us discern when we should and should not experience guilt.

Obviously, to determine when we should feel guilt, we simply turn these situations on their heads. If we failed to give our best effort, then we should face our faults and begin the process of handling guilt with honesty. If we have transgressed genuine moral standards, then we should admit our sin and accept the need for spiritual confession. If we assisted, even unwittingly, in the downfall of another person, then we should accept our complicity and seek to make amends. If we had it in our control to make a difference but didn't, then we should own up to our waywardness and begin to alter it.

When we recall the experience of George W. Truett, we discover that genuine and counterfeit guilt often wear clothing of similar colors. Only by careful discernment under the sunlight of honest appraisal can we determine which color stains our souls. When we isolate the shade, however, we begin the process of alleviating our anguish.

VII

The Scarlet Letter
The Payoff of Staying Guilty

Nathaniel Hawthorne's classic novel *The Scarlet Letter* is an age-old tale of guilt and punishment. In this story, set in mid-eighteenth-century Puritan New England, a woman named Hester Prynne finds herself pregnant out of wedlock. The Salem townspeople, strict and legalistic in their approach to life, mark the sinful Hester with a stark symbol of her fall from grace. They order her to stitch a scarlet "A" on her dress, identifying her as socially and spiritually unclean.

Resigned to her fate, Hester wears her stigma alone. Though encouraged by the town elders and even by the town minister, William Dimmesdale, to reveal her accomplice in the grievous act, Hester steadfastly refuses.

Hawthorne describes the scene in which the

Reverend Dimmesdale pleads with Hester to name her lover.

"Hester Prynne," said he, "leaning over the balcony and looking down steadfastly into her eyes....I charge thee to speak out the name of thy fellow-sinner and fellow-sufferer! Be not silent from any mistaken pity and tenderness for him; for, believe me, Hester, though he were to step down from a high place, and stand there beside thee, on thy pedestal of shame, yet better were it so, than to hide a guilty heart through life. What can thy silence do for him, except it tempt him—yea, compel him, as it were to add hypocrisy to sin? . . . Take heed how thou deniest to him—who, perchance hath not the courage to grasp it for himself—the bitter, but wholesome, cup that is now presented to thy lips!"

In spite of the minister's appeal, Hester refuses to disclose the name of her fellow adulterer. She hides her secret under the heart concealed by the scarlet letter. Through the ensuing years, she lives as an outcast in her community, loved only by Pearl, the daughter born of her ill-fated tryst.

On the other side of the spectrum, Hester's unpunished lover escapes public shame.

Tragically, however, he discovers he cannot escape his own private remorse. Though only he and Hester know his identity, the truth gradually eats away at him. His health fails, his spirit wanes, and he loses respect for himself. He wants to admit his sin and begin to cleanse his life of the guilt birthed by it, but he cannot find the moral courage to act. So, he lives a life of silent shame, adding hypocrisy to his crime of passion.

We could draw numerous lessons from this heart-touching story. One, however, etches itself most sharply in my mind. In spite of his desire to admit his guilt, Hester Prynne's lover failed to do so. Why didn't he face his transgression openly? We could say he lacked courage. He feared the consequences. He didn't want to deal with the public scorn he would suffer. As much as his guilt ate him up on the inside, he gained enough from hiding it that he refused to deal with it and cleanse it from his life.

Whether we realize it or not, many of us act much like the unknown lover of Hester Prynne. We don't always deal openly with our sin and guilt. Like Prynne's accomplice, some conflict within us keeps us from freeing ourselves from guilt's effects. Often, we gain *something* from maintaining our feelings of remorse. So, we refuse to face it and deal with it honestly.

In chapter six I said we begin to free ourselves from our guilt when we determine what type we're experiencing. Even as we identify our remorse as spawned by legitimate or illegitimate parents, though, we should accept this truth. Not everyone will face their guilt so directly. In fact, many like the Reverend Dimmesdale, will hide their pain, unable or unwilling to deal with it and gain freedom from it.

Before we can handle either type of guilt effectively, we must look at our reasons for not dealing with it squarely. We need to ask ourselves what we gain from maintaining our remorse. We must discover the emotional and spiritual payoffs that keep us from handling our pained inner selves. What keeps us from honestly dealing with our guilt?

Guilt Ties Us to a Past We Want to Keep

Several years ago I met a gray-haired, quiet woman named Florence. Something about her eyes pained me. Thin crinkles of flesh formed crow's feet on her face and made me wonder what suffering she had known. It didn't take long to find out.

I visited her at her home. Within minutes after I entered her tidy sandbox cottage, she ushered me to a bedroom in the back. It was her dead son's room. Though he had died seventeen years ago (at the age of sixteen), Florence had changed nothing in his room. A model airplane still twirled on a wire suspended from the ceiling. A picture of a high school football team sat on the dresser, surrounded by the odds and ends cherished by a teenager. His basketball shoes were perched just under his bed, like they were waiting for him to leap into them.

"You loved your son very much."

"I haven't changed a thing in this room since the accident."

"What happened to him?"

"He'd just gotten his driver's license and wanted to take the car. It was against my better judgment, but he wouldn't accept a no. So, I gave in."

Florence dropped her eyes before continuing. When she looked up again to speak, tears accompanied her words. "Two hours later the phone rang. Rick had wrecked the car. No one else was hurt but him. He'd snapped his neck. Not a mark on him, anywhere. But he was dead."

Florence waved her hand over the room, a benediction. "I'll never forgive myself for letting him take the car."

Leaving her house that day, I wondered, "Why hasn't she forgiven herself for something she couldn't help so long ago?" The answer that jumped out startled me. Florence was afraid that if she gave up her guilt she would simultaneously lose the emotional link she maintained with her dead son! By keeping her emotions so intense, she kept his memory fresh. That's why she hadn't changed anything in his room. She could still touch his belongings and therefore, touch him. To remove them threatened to remove him!

To remove her guilt might also disconnect her relationship. So, she remained tied to the past, unwilling and unable to move ahead with her present life.

Guilt Keeps Us From Dealing With the Present

Often, we refuse to deal with our guilt because we don't want to face the present moment of life. So long as we're backward oriented (remorseful over what we did) we can avoid the necessity of genuinely facing today. Guilt can keep us focused on a past event, causing us to feel dejected or angry about something we said or did. It causes us to use our present moments being occupied with feelings over the past behavior. Staying in the past keeps us from moving ahead with repentance for our actions; it keeps us from making any effort to amend our ways and reconcile with other persons; it makes it easy for us to ignore our responsibilities.

In a fascinating passage from the New Testament, the apostle Paul suggested that we "forget what lies behind and press on toward the prize for the upward call of God." In these words, Paul noted the necessity of unchaining ourselves from the past if we're to push on toward the accomplishments of the future. He suggested that we give up the past and reach out for the present and the future.

Paul had good reason for wanting to unleash himself from his past. He persecuted Christians before he became one. He had just cause for feeling guilt and not wanting to face those he had previously hurt. But, he refused to stay mired in his sinful past. He looked his former enemies in the eye, sought forgiveness from them and from the God he believed he had wronged, and stepped into his future.

We cannot move on in emotional and spiritual growth if we stay tied to the post of yesterday's guilt. But, for some of us, the guilt we feel, as painful as it is, doesn't hurt as much as the necessity of facing life's pains and the consequences of our actions.

Guilt Helps Us Manipulate Others

In my years as a pastor, I have tried to help a number of persons with addictive personalities. Typically, I've offered friendship, a listening ear, and reference points for them to find more expert treatment. Out of those experiences, I have learned that people with addictive personalities always experience deep guilt. I've also discovered that these guilty people can and will use their remorse as a tool to bend others to their wills!

It's not unusual for a pattern to emerge. Addicts indulge in their particular substance abuse. At some point, they "come to" out of their alcoholic stupor or their drug-induced high. In their normal minds again, they express morbid guilt feelings to those who seek to help them.

Typically, these expressions of guilt are genuine. But, they're also manipulative. It's hard to refuse help to those who so abjectly admit their transgressions. The person seeking to care for the addict wants desperately to believe the remorse expressed will lead to a life transformed. Sadly, however, in most situations, the remorse never leads to positive steps for change. Instead, once the abuser gets "forgiven," he or she returns to the addictive life-style.

I remember a letter I received from one young man imprisoned for crimes committed to support his cocaine habit. His words expressed well the general pattern. He wrote, "I can't believe I did such stupid things while I was on drugs. I feel so guilty for the hurt I caused. When I get out, I'm going to make a fresh start."

No doubt he meant what he said. When

prison officials freed him on parole, he went immediately to friends and family members who cared for him. He admitted his guilt and asked for their help. They responded. They helped him find a job; they loaned him money; they gave him a place to stay. Sadly, within six months he had succumbed again to his addiction.

Though probably not deliberately, he used his admission of guilt as an emotional wedge to get others to do his will. After all, how can we not forgive and offer assistance to one who so readily confesses his transgressions?

If we're not careful, any of us, even those who don't abuse drugs, can fall into a similar style of manipulation. A mother, guilty because one son went bad, can manipulate her second son to live out her dreams for him by constantly reminding him of her failure with the other boy. A child, guilty over some youthful indiscretion, can act so emotionally pained that a parent will not fulfill a planned punishment.

When we can use our guilt as an instrument to win sympathy and thus manipulate others, we may like the feeling of control so much that we won't choose to deal with the guilt itself.

Guilt Gives Us an Excuse for Our Behavior

How often have we heard someone say (as they admitted some transgression), "Well, I'm only human." This well-worn phrase often becomes an escape clause to explain away our tendencies toward illicit behavior. It gives us a handy excuse, a palatable reason for our actions. It's an admission of sin and guilt. "Yes, you caught me red-handed." But, it's also an attempt to shrug off the failure. "Yes, I'm guilty, but what else can you expect from one born and reared with this predisposition toward wrongdoing?"

With this attitude we see sin and its creation, guilt, as a by-product of a defective creative process. If we could only isolate it, we could find a tiny microbe, "the sin microbe," in our bloodstream. This genetic default creates the transgression that gives birth to the remorse. Who can blame me for the biological, inherent reality of sin?

The Psalmist said "I was conceived in sin" (Psalm 51:5). Many of us have conveniently internalized this word and distorted it to the point of saying that since we're so conceived, we cannot be expected to be anything other than a moral failure. With an inbred guilt offering us a handy excuse for illicit actions, we don't always want to remove it, lest we also lose a convenient way of explanation for our actions.

Guilt Brings Attention from Others

Though I've never witnessed the execution of a convicted murderer, I have witnessed the spectacle that surrounds such an event. In the Old West, crowds gathered at the foot of the gallows, anxious to see the condemned person hanged. In the modern world the proponents of the death penalty line up on one side of the street outside the prison while opponents stake out the other side. The death watch begins. At the appointed hour, witnesses gather outside the electrocution or poisoning chamber. Then, on the signal the executioner either pulls the switch or injects the needle. The condemned shudders for a moment, then dies.

Obviously, most of us aren't as guilty as a convicted murderer. But, our guilt can make us the center of attention in our worlds as easily as a murderer's guilt can make them the center of attention in theirs.

A school youth, feeling neglected by parents and friends at home, steals a car; he gets what he sought; his parents pay attention to him. A wife, ignored by a busy husband, indulges in an affair; she gets a double portion—attention from her lover and later from her husband who discovers her infidelity. A faceless citizen, upset that the government pays no attention to his individual complaints, attempts to kill a politician; the public trial splashes his face over the television and newspapers.

These examples perhaps represent atypical situations. But, any person who commits acts that create remorse can guarantee themselves a certain amount of attention. Also, they might not want to allay the underlying guilt in their lives for fear they won't receive the spotlight from others if they're emotionally healthy people. Branden concurred, "When I'm guilty, people will feel sorry for me."

Guilt Keeps Us From Making Painful Changes

Near the end of Hawthorne's *Scarlet Letter,* we discover the Reverend Dimmesdale was

Hester Prynne's lover. When he finally brought his guilt to the attention of the people, he unleashed forces that altered what remained of his life. From his lofty status as the holy minister, he fell to the depths of the disgraced hypocrite. Though his spirit received freedom, he experienced painful change.

Often, the fear of the changes caused by an open admission of our guilt compels us to back away from handling it. In his work, *Your Erroneous Zones,* Dyer says, "Guilt is an avoidance technique for working on yourself.... You not only avoid the hard work of changing yourself now, but the attendant risks that go with change as well. It is easier to immobilize yourself with guilt about the past than to take the hazardous path of growing in the present."

A worker steals from his company and his conscience gnaws at him. But, to deal with his remorse would mean the probable loss of his job. A wife or husband commits a momentary act of adultery and suffers the stain of the transgression. Yet, the offender knows that an admission will forever alter, if not possibly destroy, the relationship with the spouse. A teenager cheats habitually to get by in school and knows it's wrong. But, to pass without cheating means the student will need to study daily, and the pupil isn't certain it's worth that.

In the election year of 1992, Congress and the president's cabinet faced the ire of the voter because of the "Rubbergate Scandal." You recall that situation. Scores of Congressmen and a number of members of the cabinet had written bad checks at the House bank. For weeks, the shabby financial dealings were bottled up in committees. Eventually though, the facts were published. The guilty persons rushed to disclose their actions.

Not surprisingly, many voters wanted to know: "Why didn't the authorities make the information known sooner? Why did they wait until they were forced to admit their part in the scandal?" I think we can answer that question. The violators waited so long because they feared the response of the voters. They hoped they could keep a lid on the news. They feared the voters might choose someone else over them in the next election. This anxiety over the changes such disclosure might bring kept the news guarded.

Dealing with guilt will inevitably lead to changes in life-style and personal habits. So, many of us refuse to accept the risks those

changes bring. We prefer the pain in the conscience over the pain of a possible upheaval in
life.

Guilt Reinforces Our Beliefs
About Ourselves

As we've already discovered, guilt
inevitably acts as a terminator of self-esteem. It
causes us to feel bad about our personal selves.
Yet, surprisingly, many of us refuse to deal constructively with our remorse precisely because
if we alleviate it, we'll lose our sense of ourselves as "bad persons." Through our religious
training that emphasizes a God of retribution
and a humanity of despicable evil; through our
family structure with parents who continually
pound into our heads how "bad" we are;
through environmental influences at school and
in society which emphasize the negatives in us,
we accept the repetitive message.

We're convinced emotionally and spiritually
that we're bad. So, to deal effectively with our
guilt will destroy what we believe about ourselves. Thus, that process would move us out of
our comfort zone and force us to see ourselves
in a completely fresh light. Unfortunately, that

can frighten us into maintaining our fractured selves.

Recently, a young man said precisely this to me. Trying to come to grips with his self-reproach, he talked of his abusive parents. Both had failed to give him any positive support. As he said it, "My dad never talked and when mom talked it was always critical."

They had convinced him he was pretty worthless. He had internalized their opinions and found himself failing at everything he tried to do. He wanted to change that.

"You'll have to rebuild yourself from the ground up."

"That scares me."

"Why does it scare you?"

"Cause I don't know what I'll become."

Often, we decide, better a guilty self than an uncertain one.

Each of the escapes I've mentioned represent "payoffs" we receive from not dealing with our guilt. Yet, each payoff cripples us in one way or another. Each prevents us from moving ahead in grace and personal maturity.

In *The Scarlet Letter,* which I mentioned at the start of this chapter, Hawthorne describes the scene in which the Reverend Dimmesdale reveals his sin.

Partly supported by Hester Prynne, and holding one hand of little Pearl's, the Reverend Mr. Dimmesdale turned . . . to the people, . . . "People of New England!" cried he, . . . "ye that have loved me!—ye, that have deemed me holy! behold me here, the one sinner of the world! At last!—I stand upon the spot where, seven years since, I should have stood; here, with this woman. . . . Lo, the scarlet letter, which Hester wears! Ye have all shuddered at it!. . . But there stood one in the midst of you, at whose brand of sin and infamy ye have not shuddered!. . . He bids you look again at Hester's scarlet letter! He tells you, that, with all its mysterious horror, it is but the shadow of what he bears on his own breast, and that even this, his own red stigma, is no more than the type of what has seared his inmost heart! Stand any here that question God's judgment on a sinner? Behold! Behold a dreadful witness of it!" With a conclusive motion, he tore away the ministerial band from before his breast. It was revealed!

Revealed at last! He finally turned away from the reward of hiding. He openly faced his sin and guilt. It cost him. But, it also rewarded him. Only when we give up the emotional pay-offs of our guilt can we begin to gain freedom. You do seek freedom, don't you? If so, give up the guilt you still clutch to yourself.

VIII

Raising the Bar

Ways We Avoid Feeling Guilty

In October 1991, the Reverend Jimmy Swaggart found himself in desperate straights for the second time over alleged dalliances with prostitutes. The first time it happened, in 1988, Swaggart electrified the world by stepping to his pulpit on national television and confessing. With thick tears sliding down his face, Swaggart admitted he had sinned. Obviously stricken by conscience, he sought forgiveness from his family, from his followers, and from his God who watched him.

The second time he responded differently. After getting stopped by California police for driving on the wrong side of the road and for picking up a local prostitute for sexual purposes, Swaggart seemed unsure how to respond. At first, in a gesture of apparent conciliation toward his accusers, he reported he would step down from the leadership of his church and media ministries. Then, changing his mind, Swaggart appeared before his dwindling church and television audience and told them, "The Lord told me to tell you that it is flat none of your business!" Instead of remorse and confession, he responded with anger and arrogance.

Swaggart's actions demonstrate two ways of dealing with guilt. Without knowing his heart completely, but accepting his momentary sincerity, I would say that his response to his first transgression appeared proper. As we will see in more detail, confession is one of the steps to correctly handling guilt.

His response the second time, however, leads me to a different conclusion. Again, without knowing all the details, it appears that Swaggart was just as guilty of illicit behavior with the second prostitute (if you accept that a preacher shouldn't be found in *any* type of liaison with a prostitute) as he was with the first. If that's the case, then most of us would agree that he responded inappropriately the second time. Arrogantly asserting that it's no one else's business doesn't gain anyone much sympathy for weaknesses or problems.

Though we look askance at the Reverend Swaggart's continued transgressions and his inappropriate responses to them, we should admit that many of us *also* find inappropriate ways to deal with our guilts. In fact, if we're not careful, we'll find ourselves trying to flee our own stumbles in a variety of unhealthy ways. Realizing they cause us much internal pain, we'll try to cover up our hurt any way we can.

On the opposite side of the street from those who cling to their guilt and use it for emotional gain, we find those who seek to deny their guilt as a reasonable expression of their transgressions. Responding this way, however, will prevent us from actually relieving ourselves of the anguish we're trying to avoid. One key to handling guilt successfully is to face it honestly.

Though we're more subtle than Swaggart, we face the temptation of trying to pacify our conscience (or to deny it). To alleviate the psychic and spiritual pain of guilt, we must not avoid it in unhealthy ways. Yet, we try to avoid guilt in at least five ways. Before we can learn proper ways to alleviate remorse, we need to recognize the improper ways we employ to avoid it.

We Declare Ourselves Sovereign

Ultimately, only three bases for ethical decisions exist. First, we make decisions based on what we accept as a divine imperative. Second, we act upon perceived community standards of right and wrong. Third, we do what we, as autonomous moral agents, decide to do. In a typically healthy process, we will involve all of these in our choices. These three work as a triangle balancing our decisions about right and wrong. None completely suffices for a holistic view of ethics.

For instance, we can misinterpret the divine guide by misunderstanding a scriptural word, by receiving deceptive visions, or by listening to the wrong inner spiritual voices. The tragedy of Jim Jones and the mass suicides in Guyana continue to serve as the most tragic example of wrong choices made through so-called religious insight.

In a similar way, we can live by community norms. Yet, these too can go wrong. The German people yielded to the lure of communal Naziism and for centuries numbers of cultures participated in holding slaves. Even the choices of a majority can steer us to the wrong road.

That leaves us, apparently, with personal autonomy in our decision making. We must make the choice of right or wrong ourselves, as free agents, unconnected to any other moral agent or guide. We establish ourselves as sovereign masters of our ethical norms.

For anyone who seeks freedom from the ethical restraints and the resulting guilt that their faith, community, or conscience places upon them, the so-called humanist movement serves as a philosophical launching pad.

The *Humanist Manifesto* (first presented in 1933 and revised in 1973) sets forth a view of life that negates the value of traditional moral norms. The *Manifesto* sees the human being as the center of the universe; it believes that the here and now is the only realm of life ever lived; it says that scientific reason can bring total enjoyment and fulfillment to the human race; and it asserts that each person should act as a totally free autonomous agent, making his own decisions about right and wrong. Secular humanism offers everyone a complete escape from any religious restraint and allows every person the right to behave as he or she wants.

Although I would agree with the humanistic concept that individuals have value and responsibility for their actions, I cannot agree that people should exist as the sole masters of their own decisions. To do so establishes the individual as a demigod with no relationship to a divine standard of guidance. This leads to an autonomy that would destroy society as we know it. If we each make our decisions totally independent of a community norm or a divine imperative, then we inevitably face conflict with others also asserting their personal moralities. This is one way to erase guilt (or at least to decrease the number of opportunities for a person to experience it).

We end up deciding for ourselves and becoming our own judge. And, typically, most of us will find a way to declare our actions acceptable before the bar of a biased judge and jury.

We Rationalize Our Actions

Several months ago on a gloomy rainy day, I stepped to a checkout counter at a local Wal-Mart store to pay for a flashlight, a rake, two plastic trash cans, a hair dryer, and a handful of computer supplies, including paper, ribbon, and, diskettes. The checker totaled my goods and announced $66.87.

Absentmindedly, I wrote the check, picked up my bag and marched out the door. Settling in my car, I began to tally the costs in my mind. Suddenly $66.87 seemed awfully cheap. I realized something wasn't quite right.

A number of thoughts ricocheted through my head. They were holding a sale! That explained it. But I'd seen no signs. I glanced at the ticket and found the mistake. The checker hadn't charged me for the hair dryer, a $29.00 purchase. Now, the real battle began. What to do?

Take it back, obviously. But wait. The rain was pouring harder. Bring it back the next time you come. No. You'll just forget it. Why take it back at all? A chain store that large will never miss $29.00. Besides, they've probably overcharged you a few times, and you never went back to claim your money. This might even things out.

Wait a minute! You don't know that. Take it back. In the rain? Look, it will probably cost the store more in paperwork and time lost to correct the mistake than it will gain over this tiny item. Don't bother the girl and the manager with this. They'll appreciate it if you don't. Listen to yourself. You didn't pay for the hair dryer. Take it back and pay for it!

Reluctantly, I climbed out of the car, sloshed my way into the store, and settled accounts with the cashier and with my conscience. Later, reflecting on that experience, I recognized again how readily the temptation to rationalize our decisions arises in the effort to ease our guilt.

If I hadn't paid for that hair dryer, I'm certain that guilt would have raised its insistent head for a number of days, and I would have avoided that store for a while. But, gradually, given enough time and opportunity, my inner protector would have searched far afield and probably would have found a way to justify my decision (at least to myself).

Jesus once shared a parable that speaks to this normal human response. He told of a great banquet. The host has sent the invitations. But, as the story reports, "They all alike began to make excuses. The first said to him, 'I have bought a field, and I must go out and see it; I pray you, have me excused.' And another said, 'I have bought five yoke of oxen, and I go to examine them; I pray you, have me excused.' And another said, 'I have married a wife, and therefore I cannot come'" (Luke 14:18-20).

This parable teaches us one specific lesson. We know how to excuse ourselves when we don't want to respond in a certain way. We practice self-deceit as we respond in ways that violate our inner codes. Rationalizations serve as blindfolds we seek to pull over the eyes of the security guard who protects the inner conscience of us all.

We Shift Responsibility

From the beginning, the human personality has excelled in the deceit of shifting blame for inappropriate behavior. Our primordial forefather Adam, speaking to God, said, "The woman *you* gave me made me do it!" Adam pushed away his guilt by assigning it to *two* outside offenders. Not only did Eve bend his arm and force him to act rebelliously, but God ultimately deserved the blame. After all, God gave Eve to Adam.

Flip Wilson, the black comedian who brought laughter to millions in the 1970s, popularized the phrase "the devil made me do it." Unfortunately, numerous murderers and molesters have made this flippant joke line deadly serious as they have reported "voices" or "demons" ordering them to carry out heinous acts.

Often we deny our guilt by pointing a finger of responsibility at a number of influential factors. We blame our family environment; we accuse the government; or we point at the poor educational system. Others of us deny our responsibility for failure by blaming our heredity, saying that our genetic makeup made it impossible for us to choose another course of action. I like the way an anonymous poet said it:

> *I went to the psychiatrist to be*
> *psychoanalyzed*
> *To find out why I killed the cat and*
> *blacked my wife's eyes.*
> *He laid me on a comfy couch to see*
> *what he could find,*
> *And this is what he dredged up out*
> *of my unconscious mind.*
> *When I was one my mommy locked*
> *my dolly in the trunk,*
> *And so it follows naturally that*
> *I am always drunk.*
> *When I was two I saw my father*
> *kiss the maid one day,*

> *And that is why I suffer now from*
> *klep-to-ma-ni-a.*
> *At three I was ambivalent towards*
> *my younger brothers,*
> *And that's the reason why, to date,*
> *I've poisoned all my lovers.*
> *And I'm so glad since I have*
> *learned the lesson I've been*
> *taught,*
> *That everything I do that's wrong is*
> *someone else's fault.*

Obviously, heredity and environment combine to steer us in certain directions. But, we exist as more than ships, constructed out of a particular wood and pushed by a directional wind. Unlike the ship, we possess a will of our own, and that will gives us the opportunity to choose attitudes and actions. Yet, we often try to silence the voice of the conscience by shifting the blame to another's shoulders.

We Anesthetize Ourselves

Last summer I underwent surgery to repair a deviated septum, which kept me from breathing through my right nostril. It was my first time under the knife. I'll never forget the sensation of losing consciousness as the anesthetic took effect. With the IV dripping the drug into my veins, I sailed away into a happy land of relief from anxiety and pain. Through the entire two-hour process, I never felt a twinge.

Unfortunately, millions of people try to escape from their guilt in a similar fashion—masking their pain through a variety of drugs. No doctor, however, prescribes or monitors these drugs. Yet, the guilty ingest them in huge quantities in an effort to cover their emotional and spiritual pain.

Statistics tell us that 11.2 million people suffer from alcohol abuse and that another 25 million use a variety of other drugs, including prescriptions. These figures say nothing of the millions who use heroin and cocaine as a means of escape.

Though I can't say that everyone who uses drugs suffers from acute guilt aversion, the statistics and personal histories of most addicts do show that guilt serves as a strong stimulus for the individual who typically uses drugs. In my fifteen years as a pastor, I've never known a regular user of any drug who didn't suffer immensely with the demon of guilt. In fact, I believe that guilt lives as the single most prominent drive behind the compulsion to abuse any substance. People do seek to flee from facing their guilt by hiding in the stupor of a drug-induced unconsciousness.

We Raise the Bar

Several decades ago the limbo craze swept across America. You remember the dance. Two people held a pole of some kind (a broom handle, a rope, a wire) on opposite ends. A line of people waited their turn to bend their backs toward the ground and shinny under the bar feet first, then chests and heads.

After the line of people passed underneath the bar, the holders lowered it inch by inch, eliminating the people who couldn't manage to lower themselves to fit under it.

Finally, with the line stretched tightly and close to the ground, only one supple person would remain. That person won the limbo dance. The point of the dance was to gradually make it more and more difficult for people to slide under the established barrier.

In today's society not too many hosts use the limbo to spice up their parties. Maybe that's because few people want anything made more difficult for them. Instead, we want life made easier, more convenient, less taxing, and more available.

That's true in every area of life. In his work *The Baby Boomerang,* Doug Warren suggests that the current generation is the most spoiled generation in American history. The majority of people today want life at their fingertips. The success of one-stop shopping malls or stores, televisions with split screens and remote controls, shopping through catalogues, twenty-four-hour doctor's offices, drive-through funeral parlors, all demonstrate this trend.

We do want flexibility and mobility, don't we? We want the bar raised so we can pass through life easier. This isn't necessarily bad. But the desire for ease and convenience oozes into the spiritual and ethical life as well. People want flexibility and convenience in their faith and morality just as they do in every area of life.

Matters of the spirit and religion have become, in many instances, consumer oriented, seeking to satisfy the "perceived wants" of those who practice it. Not surprisingly, most of us don't want to experience anything resembling guilt. So, we devise ways of easing our consciences. We live with what I call a "Wal-Mart spirituality." We want to get what we want and not have to strive particularly hard to find it.

When we apply this to the ethical choices we make in life, we discover our desire for flexibility and convenience impacts the way we feel about such religious terminology as sin and guilt. Many want to jettison such language completely. As I heard one person say it, "I know how we can do away with all crime." I asked, "How can you do away with all crime?" The man answered, "Just declare everything legal!" We can do away with guilt by declaring everything permissible! We can "raise the bar" to the point no standard exists.

It should not surprise us when the secular person wants to reject the concept of sin and guilt. After all, if we arbitrate for ourselves the standard of right or wrong, then ultimately the only wrong is what we decide it is. Generally, we conclude what we do is okay.

When we find ourselves unable to escape the conscience or the Scripture or the voice of another that reminds us of our personal failures, we can make this final attempt to escape our guilt. We can decide to "raise the bar" and make it easier for ourselves as we "dance" our way through our ethical dilemmas.

In other words, if the standards we've formerly sought to satisfy become too difficult, if and when we transgress them, we can ease our conscience by deciding the standards aren't reasonable for us any longer. We declare them unacceptable and we rebel against their restraints.

One of the more tragic stories of the early 1990s traced the rise and fall of Mike Tyson, the former heavyweight boxing champion of the world. Tyson lived a life near the edge. He lived as he fought—with a fury and passion that overwhelmed those standing in his path.

His unchained violence carried him into numerous scrapes with the law. Finally, it carried him into a courtroom in Indianapolis, accused of raping an eighteen-year-old beauty-pageant contestant, Desiree Washington. After days of testimony, the jury reached a verdict: Guilty!

At his sentencing, Tyson denied his guilt. As he put it, he hadn't raped the girl. After all, she suffered no broken bones, no bruises, no cracked ribs. In Tyson's view, she wasn't hurt if he hadn't physically harmed her. He couldn't understand or wouldn't understand any other definition of rape. In his conscience, harm meant bodily pain.

I don't know what Tyson really thought about his actions. But, from appearances, it looked as if he avoided his feelings of remorse by raising the standard of right and wrong to a level he could walk under without emotional remorse.

We often do the same thing. We create a standard easier to follow when an old one pinches our conscience. We expand the lines of conduct if we feel trapped by the former boundaries. We make up new definitions of morality to avoid the reasonable demands of those of our past.

A recent Gallop poll demonstrates our readiness to jettison old concepts of right and wrong if they conflict with what we want to do. In the survey, people were asked to agree or disagree with this statement. "There are few moral absolutes; what is right or wrong usually varies from situation to situation." Seventy percent of respondents agreed. Only twenty-seven percent disagreed.

Given the opportunity, all of us seek ways to flee from our conscience. We widen the field of play. We flip and flop our ethical views in the attempt to escape guilt. We find destructive patterns for responding to the finger that our conscience points toward us.

In *Guilt, Anger and God,* Christopher Allison admits this can and does happen. He writes, "Our culture is, beyond doubt, beginning to deal with this problem [guilt] by lowering or even eliminating the superego material that spawns guilt.... Whether by conscious or unconscious effort, this erosion of the superego is an observable actuality, and certainly removes the problem of guilt." If this continues, we may find ourselves living in a "guiltless" society. Unfortunately, this won't necessarily mean a better society. It will mean, instead, a society which has exploded all the parameters of conduct and declared almost anything permissible.

Surely, we want to remove the pain of guilt from our lives. But, we want to do so constructively, without removing the valuable aspects of feeling the difference between right and wrong. To that effort, I want us now to direct our thoughts.

IX

Into the Shadow

Defeating Guilt—Part One

The authorities sentenced the man to die. They blindfolded him and placed him in a pitch black cave, a cave nearly one hundred yards wide and one hundred yards deep. They told him three things: 1) there was a way out of the cave; 2) if he found it he could go free; and 3) for thirty days they would provide him food and water by lowering it through a tiny hole in the roof.

The guards placed a rock over the mouth of the cave and left the prisoner alone in the dark. Pulling off his blindfold, he saw a tiny light entering the cave through the ceiling high above his head. Unfortunately, the light above added no visibility to the inky-black walls. The prisoner explored the black floor of his jail and found scattered rocks. He devised a plan. He would stack the rocks and build a mound high enough to reach the hole in the ceiling. From there he would carve an opening large enough for him to escape.

He went to work on his scheme. At the end of two weeks he had managed to build a stack of rocks ten feet high. He thought he had a chance if he could double that within two more weeks. He might reach the ceiling before his food ran out. But the rocks were harder to find now. He began to dig into the floor of the cave with his bare hands, feverishly striving to raise his mound higher. After thirty days his stack towered twenty feet high and he could almost touch the opening when he jumped. Unfortunately, it wasn't quite high enough, and he couldn't find any more rocks. For two more days he tried, jumping and falling, never quite making it. Finally, he slumped down, defeated and starved. Nine days later he died.

The next day his captors rolled the rock away from the opening of the cave, and the sunlight flooded into it. They shook their heads. Within ten yards of the opening where they stood they saw a second hole, a three-feet-wide tunnel leading into a passage that led to freedom. This was the way out that the guards had told the prisoner existed.

Unfortunately, he never explored the walls of the cavern. He had focused so narrowly on the sliver of light it never dawned on him to look for freedom in the darkness. Life waited for him all the time, not far from where he built his mound of rocks. But, to gain that freedom he had to search for it through the darkness.

What a parable for us! When we seek to free ourselves from the death caves of our guilts, we need to look for that freedom by going into the darkness. We need to admit our shameful attempts to camouflage the truth of our transgressions. We need to admit that obvious answers don't always fit us. To find the light means we need to walk first into the shadows.

As I outline this process of escape from guilt, I offer a word of caution—no one can provide a *guaranteed* way to alleviate all remorse. Indeed, as I noted in chapter five, we wouldn't want to remove entirely our sense of guilt, even if we could. We need our legitimate guilt to serve as a catalyst for change. Like a vital organ, the sense of genuine guilt acts at its best as a warning device, telling us when we have transgressed the standards we've set for ourselves or that our God has established for us.

Despite the value of legitimate guilt, we still want to decrease the painful effects it ushers into our lives. We don't want to go on feeling the edges of the sharp rock cutting into our hearts and leaving us bleeding, without joy or hope for a fulfilled life. We want to make the changes our guilt spurs us to make and move ahead—into the light of a new day—a day of freedom from our past transgressions and the self-blame they create. Plus, we want to remove the power of false remorse. We want to reject it and leave it behind us, dead and buried. We want to breathe again the air of peaceful life. How can we do this? Let's begin by examining the guilt we're experiencing.

Run Into the Guilt

As young children we enjoyed playing the game "run from your shadow." You remember how it worked. As the sun cast your slanting shadows across the ground, you tried to run away from the black form that attached itself, ghostlike, to your body. But, try as you might, you discovered no matter how fast nor how far you fled, your shadow clung to you. Only when you aged a bit did you realize you could make your shadow disappear only when you ran into another shadow. By moving your shadow into the shadows, you escaped from it.

When I speak of handling guilt, I begin by saying we cannot run from it no matter how quick our feet. Like a shadow, it attaches itself to us, clinging to our hearts and minds. Also, like our shadow, we deal positively with guilt only when we move into the darkness it casts into our lives. We move into it with courage— believing the more we understand, the easier we can triumph over the darkness in our feelings.

None of us can overcome our guilt by denying or repressing our feelings. Instead, we take the first step by accepting them, experiencing them, and then stepping beyond them. We gain the opportunity to defeat guilt only after we choose to face it and the experience which created it. When we face our guilt, we will need to do two things.

Peel the Guilt

First, we need to peel our guilt. As I said in chapter two, guilt is the residue that remains in our lives after something else creates it. Guilt lives as a feeling response to an act. Our thoughts, our responses, our attitudes (or lack of such)—all can give birth to remorse. We defeat the guilt left behind by an event only as we rigorously determine the source of the feeling. Unfortunately, we often fail to focus on that source. We never look beyond the surface emotion to see the parent of it. Yet, to gain release we have to do just that—identify the true creator of our remorse.

To defeat guilt we need to remember this truth—removing a feeling from our lives requires a process different from ceasing an action in our lives. To remove a feeling means we find out what *action* created the feeling. To stop or change an action means we discover what *feeling* initiated the action. In both cases, we're looking for the source. To correct an unhealthy feeling or an inappropriate action leads us into the shadow of our minds and spirits from which the feeling or action found its birth.

As we peel the layers of our emotions and recollections, we uncover the kernel situation that initiated our guilt. Psychologists call this process "laddering." Through it, we descend into our conscious and subconscious world, searching through the corners of the shadows, looking for the creators of our pain. We may discover the origin in ourselves, or we might find the source in another person and inappropriately placed in us. In either case, if we don't "unlayer" ourselves, we'll never know the true center of our feelings.

Consider this example. A mother finds herself feeling guilty for not signing up her eight-year-old daughter for piano lessons. All the other moms have enrolled their daughters. This mom feels unfit because she has not kept her daughter up with her peers.

At first glance this seems like a typical response for a mom who wants her child to have every opportunity for self-improvement. On further inspection, though, the mom realizes that her guilt originates from her fear of not being an adequate mother. Going deeper, the anxious mom traces her fear to her sense that she's not a good person in any regard. Finally, she gets to the center of the issue. She feels guilty because she comes from a home where she faced continual personal attacks. Her parents convinced her early in life that she possessed little value. So, she suffers from a "ladder" of guilt leading to feelings of inadequacy about her mothering skills. Only by stepping down the ladder to the bottom can we face the true cause of our remorse.

Several weeks ago, while sitting in my study, I suddenly heard the high-pitched squeal of a fire alarm. Jumping from my chair at the insistent, unbearable noise, I ran outside my office and asked my secretary to call a custodian. When the custodian arrived a minute later, I said, "Find out where that sound's coming from and shut it off!" He ran out quickly to do just that. Unfortunately for our office staff, it took him over five minutes to discover the source of the irritating blare. Finally, though, he did. He shut it off. Only when we find the source of our guilt, can we hope to shut off its shrill shriek.

Interrogate the Guilt

After we discover the source of our guilt, we should scrutinize it forcefully to determine the type of guilt we're fighting. At this point, we drag the guilt out of the shadows and look it over in the light of day. We interrogate it, demanding to know whether it's genuine or false. As discussed throughout these pages, we face legitimate and illegitimate guilt. Though the outlines of the two look similar in the shadow, if we confuse them, and make a faulty diagnosis, we'll also offer an incorrect prescription.

When we decide we're facing a fake guilt (using the standards established in chapter six), we will need to handle it differently than a genuine feeling of remorse. Typically, we fail to understand this crucial fact. If we try to care for all our guilt with one method, we will find ourselves confused and defeated. False guilt requires a different prescription than legitimate guilt. It requires a different treatment because illegitimate guilt means we're not the reason for it. Something or someone else has imposed it on us, and we've allowed them to do it. We treat guilt correctly by determining its type. Knowing the nature of our guilt, we can begin the battle to defeat it. A heartrending story from *Life* magazine taught me this lesson.

For forty-seven years no one knew the name of the blonde cherub of a girl lying in grave number 1565 in the cemetery outside of Hartford, Connecticut. She had died along with 168 others in a tragic fire that engulfed the big tent of the circus on July 6, 1944. Strangely, Little Miss 1565 suffered almost no burns on her angelic face. No one could figure out why no family member ever claimed her body.

Over the years her legend grew. Some said she was a circus orphan, with no family to claim her. Others suggested that all her family perished with her in the fire, so she had no one left to bury her. People wrote poems and songs about her. Others left notes and toy animals on her grave each year on the anniversary of her death. Someone sent fresh flowers to decorate her stone three times each year. Little Miss 1565 belonged to nobody. She also belonged to everybody.

In truth, she belonged to Mildred Cook, a white-haired, eighty-year-old lady living in a housing development for the elderly in Easthampton, Massachusetts. Mildred lived a quiet but busy life—still working part-time, active in her church, helping friends, figuring out crossword puzzles, memorizing the capitals of all the states.

Mildred desperately sought to keep her hands and mind occupied. As long as she stayed busy, she didn't have time to think. That's what she wanted to avoid at all costs.

That's why she filled her mind in her off hours with trivia—like state capitals. She didn't want to think. At times though, she couldn't push away the memories. They intruded on her, rudely. They carried her back against her will—to a hot day, four decades before, to a burning circus tent, to her frenzied effort to lead her children out of the flames.

She clutched tightly to the hand of her youngest son Edward. Her oldest boy, Donald, had already sprinted away, out of danger from the smoke and heat that threatened to over-whelm the panicked crowd. Eleanor, her eight-year-old daughter, slipped out of her sight as the frenzied crowd pushed and shoved its way out of the smoke-filled tent. Overcome by the fumes and vapors, Mildred collapsed with Edward. Her life and his were now dependent on the whims of fate.

Fate claimed Edward in death, but spared Mildred and Donald. At times later, she wished she had died too. At least death would not have left the question open. What happened to Eleanor? Mildred never saw her again. Hospitalized after the fire and unable to check for herself, Mildred left it to her sister to look for her daughter. The sister claimed she never saw her. So Mildred suffered.

She stayed busy. Idleness would give the demon memory the opportunity to gnaw at her. And memory would give the demon guilt another foothold in her spirit. Mildred often chastised herself for her failures. "Why did I take them to the circus?" "If only I had pushed and shoved, like others did." "I should've held onto her hand."

Guilt kept her active in the effort to lock such thoughts out of her mind. She survived, but not happily. She lived a tortured life, imprisoning joy behind the bars of pushy activity, afraid to look her pain in the eye.

As I read the story of Mildred Cook I couldn't help but lament, "She labored under a false guilt." Her unwillingness to examine the event under the light of reasonable expectations prevented her from removing its stain from her life. She forced herself to keep it hidden under the weight of meaningless trivia. She refused to scrutinize her pain and to consider the possibility she had done all she could, she wasn't to blame. If only she had mustered the courage to see her remorse for what it was—a genuine grief overwhelmed by an illegitimate self-blame.

When we try to escape our guilt, we will

need to see the *true character of the circumstance that gives birth to it.* We have to ask ourselves: "Did I do everything in my power to prevent this from happening?" If so, then we must see the guilt for the impostor that it is. If not, then we must honestly accept our roles in the situation and begin to work through our transgressions.

The key remains the same in either case. To defeat guilt of either type, identify the enemy! If, after identification, you decide you're suffering from an illegitimate guilt, try handling it with three steps.

Place Appropriate Responsibility

When we see we're not to blame for a particular situation, we should point the finger at the real criminal. In Chapter V, I noted we often suffer guilt stemming from the moralities of others. An ultra-conservative parent chastises a teenager for "evil dancing." A preacher blasts the women in his congregation for working outside the home and stealing time from the children. A wife blasts her husband for not working extra hours to help them build a bigger house.

I also said we often feel guilt when others blame their failures upon us. A husband accuses a wife of failing to support him sufficiently and causing him to lose a key promotion. A coach loses a championship game and chews his players out in the locker room afterward. An alcoholic wife points her finger at her family for aggravating her continued addiction.

Once we see the true character of these counterfeit creators of guilt, and once we reject them, we should reverse the responsibility and place it again upon the one who deserves it. Certainly, we should accept the responsibility when the actions of our own lives create guilt in us. But, by the same token we deserve the right to direct the responsibility to its proper source. We don't want to wear the stripes of the criminal if we didn't commit the crime!

When we identify the truly responsible party, we more clearly delineate our innocence. This requires care because we tend to place blame readily, even if it's not deserved. Also, we tend to declare our innocence, even when that's not genuine. Also, we don't place blame in the effort to punish the other person. Let their own guilt do that to them. No, we point the finger at the responsible one only to satisfy ourselves we didn't create the situation that spawned the guilt.

I'm reminded of a cartoon I saw in the "Family Business" strip recently. The mom stood in the center of the room. Her little boy stood beside a toppled table. A broken lamp rested on the floor. The mom asked: "Who broke the lamp?"

"Nobody did it!"

"It seems like your friend 'nobody' is getting into a *lot* of trouble these days."

With two daughters who also often blame "nobody," I know how this "comic strip" mom-feels. Sometimes we accuse "nobody" when we should accept the blame. In other situations, "somebody" else should get the blame and not us. In a few, nobody is directly responsible, and we should let it go at that.

Accept Your Limitations

Earlier I said we often experience a bogus guilt because of circumstances we can't control. To defeat the guilt those circumstances create, we should realize no one can control all events. So, when events cause unfortunate circumstances we accomplish nothing by taking the blame for those circumstances. Often our guilt hides a misplaced egotism. When we take on the responsibility for whatever happens to all around us, we essentially claim we're more than we are!

One fall afternoon in 1983, as I raked the leaves fallen from the branches of a towering oak in my yard, I heard the sound of a car pulling into my driveway. A junky Ford, matched by a junky-looking male driver, stopped beside me. Next to the driver sat a lady smothered with rouge. Peeking past the two in the front, I saw five scraggly children stuffed into the back seat. I guessed what the driver would say.

"Are you the preacher of the Warrenton Baptist Church?"

"Yes."

"Well, we're on the way to Florida from Virginia....I don't have no money for gas or food neither." He nodded slightly toward the backseat and lowered his voice. "We got to get these kids settled so they can get in school."

I certainly agreed with him on that, but I had been scammed too many times to give him help without trying to get more information.

"Do you have some identification?"

"No," he said. "I lost my wallet about two weeks ago. I think somebody stole it from me. I had two weeks pay in it too. That's why I'm in such a mess now. I got work waiting on me in Florida. If I can just get there.... Think you could see your way to help me...and my kids?"

Staring at those children, I knew I had no choice. He knew it too. I walked inside my house, pulled twenty dollars from my wallet and gave it to him. I thought I saw a grin play slightly on his lips as he accepted the money and backed out of the driveway. I started raking my leaves again, feeling guilty that I hadn't given him more. We often find ourselves experiencing guilt for situations far beyond our capacity to correct.

Though we should recognize the corporate nature of our national guilt (which allows the poor to fall through the cracks of our wealthy society), we need also to recognize our personal inability to change the structure as it exists. To take responsibility for all the transient people in the world places a burden on us we don't deserve. To the extent we do nothing to try and alleviate it, we deserve to feel remorse. To the extent we do what we can, but it still remains, we don't deserve the guilt that plagues us.

In the ancient Greek myth of Atlas, we meet a man who bears the weight of the whole world on his shoulders. If the world falls, he must take the blame and experience the guilt. To defeat illegitimate guilt, we will need to leave the world on Atlas's shoulders and not try to lift it completely by ourselves.

Obviously, we might find it difficult to determine when we should take responsibility for a situation and when someone else should. I've already warned against avoiding guilt by denying our responsibility. By the same token, though, don't take the blame when an unavoidable circumstance or another person deserves it.

Ask yourself these questions to determine your responsibility. Did I do anything to cause this? Have I tried to alleviate it? Is this the result of an act of nature; the result of environmental circumstances; or the result of someone else's failure? Answering these questions honestly will help us overcome illegitimate guilt.

Leave False Guilt Behind

To overcome illegitimate remorse requires us to reject it as real, to spurn it, to take power over it, and not let it dominate us into unnecessary spiritual and emotional weakness.

A favorite story of mine tells of two monks walking one morning at sunrise past a river early in the spring. Swollen with melting snows, the river had overflowed its banks and flooded the small footbridge that was the only crossing point. As the monks prepared to cross, they met a young woman. She stood forlorn by the dangerous river and asked for their help. The older monk picked her up without a word, carried her across the river and sat her down on the other side. Then, he continued his journey with the younger monk. True to their vow of sunlight silence, neither of the men said anything.

At sunset, though, when the vows of the order allowed them to talk again, the younger monk turned to his older friend and lit into him with fury. "How could you have picked that woman up? You know the vows of the order. It is forbidden even to think of a woman, much less to touch one! You have defiled yourself and defamed the order. You will need to confess and repent before all the brothers."

The elder monk shrugged his shoulders and said softly, "My brother, I put that woman down on the other side of the river this morning. It is you who have been carrying her around all day."

The elder monk refused to allow a false sin to dominate his spirit. He refused to allow it power over his life. He rejected the guilt and left it behind where it belonged. I know it's tough to do this. Often, we find it seemingly impossible, even when we emotionally and intellectually see our guilt as inappropriate. We need help to leave it behind.

Ask for Help to Overcome It

Finally, we defeat false guilt by seeking an empowerment beyond ourselves to give us spiritual and emotional freedom from it. Every release from guilt, even the irrational one, requires a spiritual energy outside of ourselves for us to overcome it. In fact, we typically need more help to combat the irrational guilt than to offset the rational one.

The person prone to false guilt usually deals with low self-esteem, which allows others to place guilt on them. Plus, the person with a low self-concept tends to take responsibility far beyond a realistic norm. This person also finds it difficult to determine objectively whether a guilt is genuine or counterfeit.

So, we need an outside source to give us guidance, encouragement, and energy. We find help from several sources. We might find it through a friend who gives us a perspective we don't gain by ourselves. Don't be afraid of going to a confidant with your guilt and asking, "Should I feel guilt over this?" A friend can possibly identify your guilt for you when you can't do it for yourself.

We might need the aid of a professional therapist if we suffer from false guilt. Sometimes religious people feel uncomfortable asking for anyone's help other than God's. Yet, just as we go to a medical doctor when a physical ailment gets serious, so also should we consider going to an emotional doctor when an inner sickness threatens to harm us.

Help can come from a book that outlines for you the two types of guilt and suggests steps to handle both. You might gain assistance from a support group at your church or synagogue or work or exercise club. In the trust circle of a group we gain several vantage points of inspection and discussion. In this setting, other people can share with you the methods they use to deal effectively with the pain of remorse.

Finally, we require assistance from our God. Though a friend can give insight and a therapist can offer counsel, only our God can provide the spiritual energy necessary to throw off the shackles of illegitimate remorse. In reality, we need the help of our God to relieve both types of guilt—illegitimate or legitimate. But, since the person who suffers from false guilt also suffers from a mistaken understanding of right and wrong, this person will require even more divine power than others. Turning to the power of the divine for assistance requires courage. It means we accept our weakness. It opens a door to the unknown. Without opening that door, we will not find the path to freedom from remorse.

To say we should turn to God for help with illegitimate guilt doesn't mean we shouldn't also seek help from these other sources. Indeed, God works in these others to accomplish divine work. Ultimately, though, if you're suffering from illegitimate remorse, you will need not only the finite help of other persons, but also the infinite help of a unique God. You will not need forgiveness (if the guilt isn't genuine, there's nothing to forgive). You will, however, need wisdom to know the difference and the power to accept the distinction.

X

Removing the Trash
Defeating Guilt—Part Two

While a youngster growing up in Greenwood, South Carolina, I joined my family in a weekly ritual. Each Saturday morning the four children loaded the trash cans from our rooms into the hallway that dissected our home. My mom then walked down the hall, pouring the small containers of trash into a larger can. When she had collected all the garbage, she carried the big barrel to the front yard. On Monday, the city collectors hauled the trash away.

That image conveys a number of implications for me. First, it reminds me guilt can bury us, like trash will, unless we deal with it periodically. Second, to rid ourselves of guilt requires us to clean it out, to remove it from our lives. Third, to clean it out, we have to "center" it, to get it into the hallway where we can't go around it or ignore it.

When I say "center" our guilt, I mean we get our faults (which cause our guilt) into a place where we can remove them. We've seen the need to run into the shadow to meet our guilts head-on within ourselves. We've seen the need to drag the guilt into the light and determine its character. When we identify our guilt as genuine, we carry it out in the following way.

Confess the Transgression

The word "confession" generally takes on religious overtones. We speak of confession to God for our sins. Even if we're not religiously inclined, however, the word still has value as we relate to the transgressions and guilt that strangle so much joy out of life. Confession means we "speak out" about our real and perceived mistakes. We accomplish this in a number of ways.

First, we can share our transgressions verbally with a friend or a counselor.

Second, we might write our sins down in a journal, noting who deserves an apology and listing ways of making amends.

Third, we could decide to make our transgressions public in the setting of our church, synagogue, or support group.

Fourth, if we believe our failure offends God, we might offer confession through prayer to the divine Lord.

Such confession helps us in two ways. It first assists in the process of asking the important question. "Is this a legitimate or illegitimate guilt?" When we confess, especially to a friend, counselor, or minister, we gain another perspective from which to see our problems. Without another view, we tend to either rationalize our guilt into nothingness or to magnify our supposed failures into giants of undefeatable proportions. Bringing our guilts into the light of confessional scrutiny enables us to see the genuineness of the enemy we're fighting.

Confession also helps by giving us a way to purge our internal rooms, to carry the garbage out of our systems. Much like a cluttered room that needs clearing before it can sparkle again, our lives get cluttered up by the garbage of our transgressions. Confession, used carefully, acts as a spiritual and emotional "cleanser," carrying the unwanted mess of our guilt out of us. It represents a movement, a shift, a transfer of the guilt within us to a place beyond us. Confession means we get the trash in the hallway. From there we can put it in the larger can for dumping.

To facilitate confession, we should do three things.

1. Make your confession concrete. Write it down. When the police pick up suspects for a crime, they seek a confession from them. They tape-record interviews. If they get the suspects to admit an offense verbally, they then also get them to sign a document attesting to their deed. In other words, they make it concrete!

   We make our confessions concrete as we verbalize specifically (to others, to God) where we think we failed. Don't generalize! Be specific. We make them concrete as we "journal" our daily lives. We make them concrete as we go to the person or persons offended and admit our sin against them.

   A confession by its nature moves guilt beyond us. It symbolizes the action of getting it out. It conveys a transference from within us to outside of us.

2. Make your confession sooner rather than later. The longer we hold a guilt within, the more difficult it becomes to go to the person, to admit our failures, to accept our responsibility. The farther away from an action or inaction we get, the stronger the temptation of rationalization becomes. We bury our guilt under the weight of days, which pass between the time we err and the time we admit our waywardness.

3. Make your confession symbolically. Though I am of the Protestant faith, I have always seen a strength in the Catholic system of confession. A guilty person goes to a priest, admits the sin, and supposedly leaves the guilt in the booth. Though I don't accept the need for a priestly mediator, I do accept the need for a symbolic act of confession. You could go to a church and kneel at the altar before God. You might write your sin down and place it in your Bible. You could burn the paper. Or tear it into

tiny bits. You could stand outside and raise your arms skyward and air your waywardness to the Almighty. A symbolic gesture aids our confession.

Take Responsibility for The Transgression

When we confess, we admit that guilt exists within us. We gain the opportunity to scrutinize the cause and determine its legitimacy. If we decide we have sinned, then we go another step. We accept the fault for causing the situation that created the guilt. It is one thing to say, "I feel guilty." It is still another to say, "I acted in such a way that I *should* feel guilty!"

Even if we confess we did it, we could still blame another person or some circumstance for our failure. We can't get over guilt if we never accept our part in causing it. To find relief from rational guilt, we take personal responsibility as the creators of it. We uncover the sin, we bring our failure into the light of day, we specifically admit the error that caused us to feel guilty. In the language of the twelve-step recovery process for addictive behaviors, we "take a fearless inventory of our lives."

In this step we stop blaming anything—

heredity, environment, God, the devil, or another person—for our transgressions. We accept our responsibility and refuse to hide behind the facade of excuses. We get honest with ourselves and hold up our failures for personal scrutiny. Once we confess and accept responsibility, we can move to the next phase of recovery.

Expunge the Transgression

As March 6, 1992, approached, the world waited with bated breath to see if the dreaded "Michelangelo" computer virus would wreak as much havoc as the experts predicted. You might recall that situation. According to reports, the virus would infect millions of IBM and IBM compatible computers and destroy the data stored on the hard and floppy disks in the systems. As a computer user, I felt a reasonable concern my system would fall prey to this blight. To protect myself, I called a friend who works daily with computers and asked him what to do. Paul said, "Don't worry about it. I'll come by tonight and make sure you're protected."

True to his word, he came by about seven P.M. He brought with him a scan program to check out my system and see if I had caught any virus. Wouldn't you know it—I had! But not Michelangelo. I had one called "KeyPunch."

My friend didn't desert me. Instead, he produced another package. He programmed it onto my hard disk and it went to work, deleting the invader. This cleansing program acted like an injection into a dread disease and wiped out the virus. What a relief! To cleanse my computer system, I did two things. First, I admitted I couldn't handle the situation myself. I needed help. Second, I specifically asked someone more capable than myself to come to my aid. Removing the pain of guilt forces us to follow a similar process.

Admit Our Inability to Remove the Guilt

To cleanse our life systems from the guilt that threatens to destroy us, we too will need to admit our need for assistance. This requires courage and places us at risk. As people taught to hide our weaknesses, any sign of insufficiency can cause others to see us as weak. It can cause us to question our own strength. We think, "Shouldn't I manage my own problems?"

Yet, amazingly, we ask for help in practically every other arena of life. We go to a medical doctor for treatment of physical ailments. We call a plumber when our commode stops up. We set up golf lessons with the club pro when we want to improve our golf game.

Why the sudden shame and reluctance to admit our inability to handle our emotional and spiritual problems? We're no more an expert in those fields than in the ones I've just mentioned, are we? Yet, we often refuse to admit our need for help—to ourselves or to anyone else. Unless we do, though, we won't free ourselves from the emotional and spiritual ailment of remorse.

Ask for Help to Remove Our Guilt

Significantly, not only did I admit my need for help to remove the computer virus, but I also asked someone to come to my aid. I called Paul on the phone; I invited him over to my house to check my system; I gave him free reign to work on my computer so he could fix it. Asking opened the possibility of receiving the assistance I desperately required.

We can know our incapacity to cleanse ourselves, but if we never make the call for another's guidance, we will never make ourselves available for it. That assistance may take a variety of forms. A friend we've wronged may pick up the pain in our suffering conscience and carry it away in an act of forgiveness. A counselor may direct us toward a therapy method that will purge us of our suffering. A minister might lead us to understand our personal value, in spite of our sin.

Ultimately, if we're going to bury our guilt in a proper grave, we require the assistance of the divine. Although we might follow all the correct physical steps of verbal confession, although we might follow all the correct emotional steps of crying or cursing or counseling, I don't personally believe we can remove the stain of our hurt without the help of a power beyond ourselves. Our friends can't encourage without our willingness to let them. God won't cleanse what we don't open to the divine grace.

Again, the Twelve-Step Program uses language similar to this as it offers help to the substance abuser. In steps two and three, individuals accept a Power greater than themselves as necessary for healing. They place themselves in the care of this Power. Step seven continues the emphasis on the divine as it encourages the individual to "humbly ask God to remove our shortcomings."

Obviously, the Twelve-Step Program leaves the concept of God open to every person's interpretation. I personally accept the manifestation granted to us in the person of Jesus as recorded in the Judeo-Christian scriptures. Though the nature of our God might differ, the need for God's help in cleansing guilt remains the same.

In a heartrending Psalm we hear King David admit his sins. He said, "I know my transgressions and my sin is ever before me." Then, he called out for divine help. "Purge me with hyssop," he cried, "and I will be white as snow." David saw his failures. He confessed them. Then, he pleaded with God to remove them from his life. He begged, "Create in me a clean heart, O God, and renew a right spirit within me." When we ask, God acts faithfully to cleanse us of our sin and the guilt created by it.

Ask For and Receive Forgiveness

I've not said anything yet in these pages about forgiveness. Without it, though, none of us will find our way off the street of our guilt trip. We can confess to ourselves we've broken our personal codes. We can confess to those we've hurt. We can confess to God we've shattered the divine standards. But confession by itself doesn't remove guilt. Confession begins the process, but guilt requires a tougher soap than that. Only forgiveness cleanses away the stain that covers our hearts.

Years ago, in the dark ages of black-and-white television, viewers often saw commercials for Lava soap. In those advertisements, a burly man entered the bathroom after a hard day's work. His hands, held up for all to see, were covered with grease and grime. The announcer then proclaimed: "Only one thing will get these hands clean! L-A-V-A!"

Stained by the real and perceived failures of our lives, we stand before each other and before the God who made us. From offstage we hear the pronouncement: "Only one thing will get these lives clean! Forgiveness!"

Where do we seek this forgiveness?

Forgiveness from Others

First, we seek it from others. We go to the ones we've offended and ask them to unchain us from guilt through the grace of their forgiveness. Corrie Ten Boom, a Jewish Christian, spent time in a Nazi prison camp during World War II. After the allied victory and her release, she traveled through Europe preaching the power of forgiveness. One Sunday, in Munich, Germany, after she had preached a sermon on forgiveness, a man hurried over to her and held out his hand, expecting her to take it. She didn't.

He said, "Fraulein Ten Boom, I am glad you teach the power of forgiveness." She knew what he wanted. He wanted her to forgive him. But, she couldn't. She recognized him. She remembered how she was forced to take showers, with other women prisoners, while this beast looked on, a leering, mocking "superman," guarding helpless naked women. Corrie remembered. He put his hand close to her. Her own hand froze at her side.

She could not forgive. She was stunned and terrified by her own weakness. What could she do, she who had been so sure that she had overcome the deep hurt and the desperate hate and had arrived at forgiving. What could she do now that she was confronted by a man she could not forgive?

She prayed. "Jesus, I can't forgive this man.

Forgive me." At once, in some wonderful way that she was not prepared for, she felt forgiven. Forgiven for not forgiving. At that moment—in the power of the feeling—her hand went up, took the hand of her enemy, and released him. In her heart she freed him from his terrible past. And she freed herself from hers.

This man did what we also should so. He went to the one whom he had offended and sought forgiveness. The person might not forgive us. But, if not, we have gone as far as we can. We leave it with them as their spiritual problem and not ours.

Forgiveness from God

Second, we seek forgiveness from God. For people of faith, sin has eternal consequences. It requires eternal solutions. Thankfully, faith tells us of a God who stands in readiness to offer forgiveness to us. The scriptural word says, "If we confess our sins, he is faithful and just to forgive us our sins and to cleanse us from all unrighteousness" (1 John 1:9).

The word *forgive* means God scrapes from our lives the stain of our rebellion against the divine way. God declares the criminal not guilty. God remembers our transgressions no more.

When my friend Paul used a cleansing package to take the virus from my data files, I didn't ask where the virus went. I don't know what happened to the computer disease that threatened to destroy the usefulness of my machine. It simply disappeared, vanished, never to return. Forgiveness works the same way. God cleanses our lives. God treats us as if we had never sinned, as if no disease had ever invaded us. God acquits us as if we had never committed a crime. God "makes us right," not out of our own merit, but out of the abundance of divine grace.

Unfortunately, many of us want freedom from our guilt but refuse to turn to God for the forgiveness that will make it possible. We reject God because we think of religious faith as a guilt-producing agent of life. For centuries, the critics of religious faith have portrayed its essence as condemnation, as a system of rules and a code of laws that cause us grief of conscience when we break them.

The biblical image for this perspective arises from the picture of banishment recorded in Genesis 3. God shut the human race out of the Garden because of sin. Then, God placed guards at the gates to protect the divine domain. In this depiction of religion, God acts primarily as a judge who excommunicates us from Paradise.

Yet, that image fails to understand the concept of the gospel as "good news." It fails to look to the New Testament picture of God as a parent who seeks to embrace each person.

The New Testament image springs from a touching story Jesus told. In Jesus' parable we meet a young man who decided to take his share of his father's wealth and leave home with it. The boy settled in the big city and instantly embraced the nightlife available there. He wasted his father's money on fast women and fancy cars. Within months he was broke. Worse still, he was alone. The friends who flocked to him while he had money have fled.

The boy, in despair, saw the error of his ways. Humbled, he decided to go home. On the way, he wondered if his father would take him back. After all, he sinned against his family. He was guilty of pride and greed and ingratitude and wastefulness. Why should they take him back?

With his fears, he hitchhiked home. If

nothing else, his father would give him a job on the farm. He could work close to home, even if he couldn't live there as a son any more.

Worn out and defeated, he arrived at the corner of the street near his home. He stood there, scared to go further. To his amazement, he saw his dad on the porch looking at him. His father jumped down the steps and ran to him, arms open, tears flowing down his face. His father embraced him tightly, laughing and shouting—all at the same time, welcoming him home. His father called all the neighbors, he threw a festive party, he treated the wayward son like a conquering hero. He forgave him. He loved him. He restored him as a son. Jesus taught that God responds to us like this loving father.

Here we see the true image of Christian faith. We see not an armed cherubim guarding the gates to joy, but an anxious father running down the road, eagerly embracing the wayward child. We hear not excommunication and guilt, but restoration and forgiveness.

The New Testament word says, "There is no condemnation to them that are in Christ Jesus" (Romans 8:1). No matter how we view it, the Christian Gospel teaches us Jesus ventured into our world not to produce guilt but to proclaim grace. He stepped into the streets of our society not to pronounce condemnation, but to offer forgiveness.

Maybe your faith expresses it in different terms. But, even if our terms differ, we need to accept this truth; we need to ask for divine assistance to heal our sin and remove our guilt.

The man with the filthy hands in the Lava commercials picked up a bar of soap off the sink, and the suds washed the grease away. We take up the word of God's acquittal and the grace found in those words washes our guilt into the redeeming love of the divine.

Forgiveness for Ourselves

Earlier in this chapter I used the analogy of removing trash to describe what we do to remove genuine guilt. I want to take that analogy one step further. Even after we carry our trash to the street or off to the landfill and even after we accept help from someone else to bury it or to burn it, we will probably find some residue remaining in the containers we keep: a piece of old candy, glued by the syrup to the bottom of the can; a piece of paper wedged into the corner; a slice of browned banana pasted to the side. The can remains contaminated by bits and pieces of our refuse.

In spite of what we believe about God's forgiveness many of us continue to struggle with guilt sticking to our lives. We continue this struggle largely because *we haven't yet managed to forgive ourselves.* I've heard this refrain over and over. A person says, "I accept that God forgives me. But, I haven't been able to forgive myself."

Probably, no matter what I say here, we will always fight the battle for self-forgiveness. We will fight it because we continually transgress our internal codes and our conscience always stands ready, making plain our sin. We will fight it because we're constantly struggling against our inferiority—finding it tough to accept that God could love us so deeply as to acquit us of our crimes. We will fight it because we're always combatting doubt—disbelieving that God does exist and has the power and the will to enact forgiveness for us.

In the midst of these pitched battles, however, we seek a victory over our lack of forgiveness for ourselves. For us to finally stop the guilt trip we have to get off the one-way street of self-condemnation. We have to learn to forgive ourselves. We have to cleanse the cans of our hearts. Let me offer three keys to self-forgiveness.

Recycle the Transgression

Generally, we think of "garbage" as something we immediately throw away. Yet, in the years since my childhood, that concept has changed considerably. Now, we often find ourselves recycling what we once perceived as useless waste. When we recycle, we take something we thought had no more purpose and use it to make something of continuing value. When we deal with the difficult problem of forgiving ourselves, we find it necessary to do something similar. We can't forgive ourselves simply by saying we will. We can't talk ourselves into it. So, we have to take a negative and turn it into a positive.

Guilt makes us feel less than good about ourselves. It traps us into a sense of personal failure. Forgiving ourselves means we get a new vision of our value. We begin to like ourselves. We accept our sinfulness, but we reject our sinfulness as the only possibility for us. We reject the notion that we're doomed to always doing evil. We decide to do something good. We act positively toward those we've hurt; we recycle our transgressions and create a fresh feeling about ourselves.

After confessing our failures and seeking forgiveness for them, we tend to think that will end our struggle. But, typically, that's not enough to gain forgiveness from our inner judge. Instead of glibly trying to wish away or think away our guilt, we remove it more completely by "recycling" it into ministry and service for others. The language of Twelve-Steps calls for us to make this type of effort as we make either direct or indirect amends for the hurts we caused through our addictions. We use identical language in regard to the past mistakes that create our guilt.

We "recycle" guilt by offering reparation for the wrongs we've committed. If at all possible, we deal directly with the person whom we have hurt. We apologize, we return a stolen item, we donate time or money to a cause or an institution. When we can't make direct reparation, we act through the community to provide a service or ministry to enhance the greater good.

In the movie *Gandhi,* which played to

packed houses across America several years ago, a Hindu man approached the Indian prophet one day with a dark guilt burdening his spirit. In a fit of rage over the death of his own son at the hands of a group of Muslims, the man had killed a Muslim boy. He told Gandhi, "I am in hell."

Gandhi offered him a way out of hell. He advised the man to find a Muslim orphan and raise the boy as his own child. But, instead of teaching the child Hinduism, Gandhi told the man to raise him in the tenets of the Muslim faith. Only, then, said Gandhi, could the man find the power to forgive himself.

Gandhi's advice speaks to us all. To forgive ourselves of our guilt, we must recycle it in service and restoration. This effort "to make up" for our transgressions will fail if it's designed to "earn" a forgiveness for our failures. Indeed, no one can pile up such merit as to remove all their mistakes. The effort "to make up," however, does give us a sense of personal well-being, which proves valuable to us as we seek to cleanse our emotional and spiritual veins of the plaque called guilt.

We consistently discover the concept of reparation in the biblical writings. One story describes a diminutive man named Zacchaeus. A Jewish tax collector, Zacchaeus cheated his kinsman for his own ill-gotten gain. One day Zacchaeus encountered Jesus and his misguided life made a turn for the better. As evidence of his relationship to Jesus, he declared, "If I have taken anything from anyone by false accusations, I restore fourfold."

Jesus understood and accepted the emotions that compelled Zacchaeus to act this way. For him to regain his self-respect he had to make amends for his previous sin. Reparation leads to self-forgiveness.

Decide to Respond Differently

To forgive ourselves also requires us to choose a different response to a similar situation in the future. If we know that an act (or a failure to act) in the past caused us remorse, but do nothing to alter our response in the future, then the guilt will never leave us.

I recall visiting with a young woman several years ago who found herself facing this dilemma. She tugged on the straps of her purse as she talked. She asked me: "If a person is doing something they know is wrong, will God forgive them?"

"Does that person plan to keep on doing what they know is wrong?"

"I don't know."

"When that person knows, come back to me and ask me that question again."

I knew her situation. She was "that person." She was living with a young man in spite of her background in the church, which caused her to feel her actions were wrong. So, she suffered from painful guilt. Yet, she hadn't decided if the pain of the guilt hurt more than the pain of giving up the situation that created it. Until she changes her way of response, she will never forgive herself and defeat her sense of remorse. To use our garbage analogy, we can't get the garbage out of the house if we decide we want to keep it in our room!

Harlan Weschler, a Jewish writer and teacher, relates a helpful story. Every night Levi Yitzhak, an elderly Jewish rabbi, reviews the events of the day just passed. He identifies the evil he has committed in it. Then, before he goes to sleep he pledges, "I shall not do this again." Each day he follows the identical pattern. He reviews his day and identifies his sin. He declares, "I shall not do this again." And, each night he says to himself, "But you promised that last night and the night before." Each time he responds, "Yes, but this time I mean it." To forgive ourselves requires us to labor daily to respond in ways different from our previous choices. By gaining control of our responses in the future, we gain freedom from our guilt of the past.

Rejoice in the Possibility of Re-Creation

To forgive ourselves we also need to believe in the possibility of personal re-creation. Sin and guilt often lead us to a point of despair about ourselves. We fall into such discouragement we cease to believe in the possibility of changing our feelings or our responses in the present or the future. We end up not forgiving ourselves because we think we'll always stay the way we are.

But we need not remain in such a state. Instead, we can hear again the divine word of transformation. If religion teaches us anything (and I mean any religion), it teaches us we can change. Indeed, every religion of which I'm aware, teaches us the necessity of change for us to fulfill the divine will for our lives. If we don't believe we can experience transformation, then we will see no need and no purpose in trying to purge ourselves of past transgressions. If we can't live differently than in our past, then why worry about our past failures.

I want us to hear the word of re-creation. We can live different lives. As we live transformed lives, we discover the path of forgiveness for ourselves. By seeing ourselves making good choices in the present, we gain the power to forgive ourselves for bad choices in the past. I don't know of a more powerful tonic for a person sick of guilt than to believe they can start over, they can experience re-creation of spirit and life.

I want to conclude this chapter with the story of a hate-filled man who completely changed the direction of his life.

In July of 1987, forty Jewish families in Phoenix, Arizona, received a series of phone calls from a man promising them he would finish the job that Hitler had started. Within weeks, Phoenix police traced the despicable calls to a young, unemployed tree-nursery worker named David Waughtal.

Waughtal, a no-account failure at everything he had ever started, had fallen gradually under the sway of neo-Nazi groups. Under their influence, he blamed all of his problems on Jewish conspirators who supposedly caused all of the evils of American society. Out of frustration, Waughtal had grown angry, and the calls he made to the innocent Jews demonstrated his rage.

Then, the police arrested him. Before he went to trial, though, Waughtal fled. He ended up in Oregon with his grandmother. He took a job in a lumber mill and continued his downward slide.

One night, under the influence of alcohol, he ran his car off the road and ended up in jail. That episode shook him up, and he realized he had to change his life. Through the influence of a minister who befriended him, Waughtal recognized the error of the teachings of the neo-Nazis. He also made a decision to follow the teachings of Jesus.

Following his conversion he decided that he needed to seek forgiveness from those he had wronged if he was ever to know genuine peace. With the help of his minister, he called Joel Breshin, head of the Phoenix office of the Anti-Defamation League of B'nai B'rith, and asked his forgiveness. He then began a remarkable process, going to each court where crimes were lodged against him and pleading guilty to each charge. He also visited every Jewish family he had called that he could find and asked for their forgiveness.

As Rabbi Bill Berk described, "I was very skeptical until one Friday night when this young man came and sat through the whole service. When it was over, he came up to me, eyeball to eyeball, and said, 'I want to ask you forgiveness.' I thought, 'This is for real. This is a remarkable man.'"

The David Waughtal story gives us one example of a man who dealt successfully with his transgressions and the guilt that followed them. He faced his wrongdoing; he sought help to change; he turned himself in a new direction with the aid of others and the divine; he sought to make direct amends where possible; he decided to respond differently to the situation at every possible opportunity; he continues to seek reconciliation and renewal; he has learned to forgive himself. Under the grace of our God, so can we.

XI

Searching for the Holy Grail

Living Beyond Guilt

The ancient legend of King Arthur and the Knights of the Round Table continues to inspire us with its timeless message of courage and valor. Of all the tales this legend has generated, none so captivates my imagination as the search for the Holy Grail.

The quest for the Grail, the cup from which legend says Jesus drank at the Last Supper, consumed the Knights of Arthur's Table. They believed the cup possessed spiritual powers. It could heal the body and the soul of all afflictions.

The good knight Percivale, in Tennyson's poem, spoke of its wonder. "If a man could touch or see it, he was heal'd at once, by faith, of all his ills."

Driven by the desire to "touch or see" the Cup which could cure the ills of life, the Knights of the Table swore an oath to find it. King Arthur warned them the pursuit would bring hardship and even death. He said, "Many of you, yea most, return no more."

In spite of the king's dire prophecies and their own fears, the urge to find the Grail compelled the knights to the quest. They ventured out, into the realm, to the far reaches of civilization. For years they searched, enduring hardships beyond measure. They split up, going their separate ways, accepting loneliness—all for their desire to find the healing chalice.

Years later the survivors of the quest returned. Of those who left, only three, Sir Galahad, Sir Bors, and Sir Percivale ever "saw" the sacred cup. Percivale described the vision of the bloodred cup, "I saw the Holy Grail.... And in the strength of this I rode, shattering all evil customs everywhere.... And broke thro' all, and in the strength of this, come victor."

The story of the Grail continues to attract us because it represents our search for a way out of the problems of life. We too want healing—from the physical, emotional and spiritual wounds we experience. We also want to "come victor" and find a Paradise of contentment.

The quest symbolizes the drive we share to discover a quiet place of reconciliation with our inner selves, with our fellow persons, and with our God. It represents our quest for an escape from the accusing finger of our hurting conscience. It represents our desire to find a land beyond the ravages of remorse.

In these pages I've suggested a method to help us deal with our guilt in a healthy, self-enhancing way. In a sense, we've been on a search for a Holy Grail, for a healing Cup of faith and understanding we can "ingest" into our lives. Hopefully, even if we haven't found the Grail yet, we've at least walked forward a few steps on the journey.

As we continue the trek, we face one final issue. What will we find if we grasp the Cup? What happens in the land beyond guilt? What takes place if we get off the dead-end street of illegitimate guilt and the one-way street of unrealistic remorse? What difference will it make in our lives if we can find a way to handle our guilt reasonably, learning from it when it's legitimate and freeing ourselves from it when it's not?

I think the Cup will heal us in five ways.

An Appropriate Appreciation for the Self

If guilt destroys self-esteem, as we know it does, then an honest acceptance of our failures and a careful handling of them cannot help but lead us into a deeper appreciation of our own strengths.

When we feel guilty, we find it difficult, if not impossible, to believe we have any value. We can't accept love from anyone. The word *love* jars us because we can't believe anyone would speak it of us. In the land beyond guilt we will hear and accept the word of love for ourselves and understand our true value again.

I don't mean we will unrealistically puff ourselves up as though we live without fault. I do mean we will appreciate ourselves as persons of intrinsic worth, of inherent value, and of genuine dignity in spite of our waywardness.

In those lovely words which so many of us know, the Scriptures say, "God showed His love for us, in that while we were yet sinners, Christ died for us." These words remind me: I have fallen short of the divine ideal; God loves me in spite of my sin. In his moving book *Why Me: Coping with Grief, Loss, and Change,* Pesach Krauss describes the torment of his youth. Having suffered the amputation of the lower half of his right leg, he felt incomplete. Desperately wanting to fit in with others, he pushed himself to achieve. Wearing a prosthesis he participated zealously in athletics. He refused any pity. Through sheer determination, Krauss made the gymnastics team his sophomore year and earned a letter. Later, he remembered the first day he wore the sweater to school.

The kids stopped their chatter and turned to stare at me....A hush came over the room. And then an amazing thing happened. In unison, all my classmates rose. They began to clap their hands....And they cheered.

I'm not ashamed to tell you that on that day, standing there in front of my classmates, the tears I cried were the sweetest tears of all.

For the first time I had a glimmer that I could be a whole person even if part of me is missing.

Not a single one of us stands completely whole in body, mind, or spirit. We're imperfect and incomplete. Yet, even with our imperfections, we are valuable. When we grasp the Holy Grail, when we move beyond forgiveness into acceptance, we grasp the ambiguity of the good and the evil within ourselves. We don't gloss over our sinfulness, but neither do we allow our sinfulness to mask over our sense of value and worth.

No matter how despicable our deed, no matter how low we sink, we cannot escape this truth—our God cares for us, our God loves us, and we find our worth in that divine love. Knowing this, we can look into the mirror each morning and see, not a perfect person, but not an entirely useless person either. Having accepted responsibility for our transgressions, having confessed our wrongdoing and wrong-being, having made restitution and reconciliation where possible, we can shake our heads in acknowledgment that though moral perfection isn't ours, total depravity isn't either. So, we can allow ourselves the privilege of loving and accepting ourselves.

A Rediscovery of Innocence

Not too long ago I stopped by the hospital to visit with a young woman in my congregation who had recently given birth to an eight-pound baby boy. After spending a few minutes with the mom and dad, I excused myself and headed for home. On the way out, I walked past the nursery. I looked through the clear glass window and saw eleven newborn children—four boys and seven girls. I pressed my nose against the window. A nurse saw me and waved, thinking I was a new father. I waved back, wishing a little she was right.

Standing and staring at those babies, I found myself thinking, "How innocent they are!" No black marks against them. No mistakes. No failures on their report cards. No sin. No guilt!

Wouldn't you like to return to that innocent state? In one way, no one can. Children live in ignorance, and that ignorance leads to innocence. They don't know enough to feel guilt. They don't know the rules, so they haven't broken any.

We do know the limits. We have transgressed them. So, we feel guilty. Yet, our faith tells us we can experience a clean slate. We can walk again through virgin forest. Though our sins are as crimson, they shall be as white as snow.

In Joan Borysenko's engaging book *Guilt is*

the Teacher, Love is the Lesson, she quotes a passage under the picture of a girl in her son's high school yearbook. The young lady wrote: "When I was so young, it seemed that life was so wonderful, a miracle, it was beautiful, magical. But then they sent me away to teach me how to be sensible, logical, responsible, practical. Won't you please tell me what I've learned?"

Maturity brings responsibility. Unfortunately, with responsibility comes guilt. By responding carefully to our guilt, though we can regain a portion of the beauty of our childhood.

On one occasion in the New Testament, a group of children gathered around Jesus. The disciples, hoping to protect Jesus from the bother, tried to push the children away. Jesus surprised them with his response. He said, "Unless you repent and become as little children, you shall not enter the kingdom of God" (Matthew 18:3).

Scholars have long debated what Jesus meant in these words. Did Jesus mean we have to return to the ignorance of children? Did he mean we should return to the humility of children? Did he call us to return to the trust level of children? Maybe he meant each of these, based on the need we have in our personal lives.

I believe he meant we have to return to the innocence of children, to the guilt-free state of life children enjoy. That makes sense. If we're to enter the kingdom of heaven, beginning now, we have to receive forgiveness and find reconciliation with others and with God. We receive forgiveness and remove our guilt at the same time. When God forgives us, when others forgive us, and when we forgive ourselves our guilt disappears. We become children again, fit for the kingdom of God.

A Discovery of Inner Peace

In the first chapter I told the story of the bridge over the Kwai River. Briefly, recall the situation. During World War Two thousands of Allied prisoners died under the hands of their Japanese captors who forced them to build a 250-mile railway across the Kwai River in Thailand. In that chapter, though, I didn't tell you the rest of the story. In 1990, almost fifty years after the original atrocities of the slave-like conditions, people living near the former bridge site still found themselves fighting the old fears. One man who lived near the ruins of the prison camp found himself having trouble sleeping. Sompong Chorenchai, a motorcycle repairman, reported to his friends that his dreams "were haunted by ghosts."

He saw mass graves and many bodies in his dreams. After weeks of such misery, Chorenchai sought out a friend named Ananya Watanayam, who owned land less than a mile from the Kwai River. Sompong learned the farmer had found human bones in the soil near his farm. With Chorenchai's urging, local authorities explored the area near the railroad tracks. While digging, they found a mass grave containing the skeletons of over five hundred prisoners. Some of them had their skeletal hands tied with wire. Apparently, many of them were buried alive.

Again at Sompong's urging, the authorities collected all of the remains from the pits. Then, local Chinese and Thai monks performed religious rituals to bring peace to the troubled souls who had lain there. After these rites were completed, Sompong Chorenchai reported his dreams disappeared. He could sleep well again.

All of us who experience guilt want to "sleep well again." We want the disharmony in our spirits quieted. We seek a slowing of our anxious hearts and a stilling of the troubled waters churning inside. When we appropriately handle our guilt, we will rediscover the freedom to sleep again without the disturbing dreams that haunt us. The troubled waters of the heart will fall quiet, and we will know peace.

A Freedom to Embrace and Care for Others

In his novel *Crime and Punishment,* the Russian novelist Dostoevski described the desperate struggle of a killer named Ilyon Raskolnikov. Ilyon had killed an elderly woman without just cause. Driven by guilt, he revealed his act to Sonia, an angelic girl who had fallen in love with him. With her guidance, he confessed to the police. After trial, the court sent him away to Siberia for punishment.

The lovely Sonia followed him there, hoping he could find a way to forgive himself and to love her. Ilyon went through hell, trying first to rationalize his actions. He refused to blame himself, preferring instead to blame fate, to blame circumstances, to blame anything but himself. To accept his guilt, he thought, meant to accept his total depravity.

Finally, he couldn't ignore it any longer. He recognized the deception within himself. He accepted his responsibility. He admitted his sin.

Amazingly, in the same instant he confessed, he found himself free to love Sonia as she loved him. He threw himself at her feet in an act of desperate embrace. Freed of guilt he found freedom to love.

Guilt separates us from others. It erects barriers between those we want to embrace, those we seek to appreciate and love. It pushes us into our own private hells and leaves us lonely for the warmth of another's embrace.

By moving beyond guilt, we regain the opportunity to build loving relationships with people around us. We give up the anger that consumes us, the self-hatred that makes us feel unworthy of another's care and the pain that prevents us from feeling it when another reaches out for us. In the land beyond guilt, we drink again from the cup of human companionship and find a renewal of relationship.

A Restoration with Our God

In the New Testament we meet a man consumed at the core by guilt. Perhaps you recall the story. Simon Peter had followed Jesus into the courtyard of Herod on the night the authorities arrested the Nazarene.

Standing outside, warming his hands by the fire, Peter waited to know Jesus' fate. A young girl watched him closely in the glow of the flames. Thinking she recognized him as one of Jesus' companions, she asked, "Aren't you one of his followers?"

Fearful of his own fate, Peter quickly denied a relationship with Jesus. "I am not."

Others standing at the fireside joined with the girl and questioned him a second time. "Aren't you one of his followers?"

Again, Peter denied it. "I don't know the man."

A third time, the group pressed him. Finally, exasperated and angry, probably at himself more than anyone else, Peter cursed, swore an oath of denial, and fled from the scene.

We don't know where Peter ran. He disappears for a couple of days from the biblical narrative. We don't see him again until the morning of the reported resurrection of Christ. He resurfaces when Mary Magdalene, one of the female followers of Jesus, proclaimed an astonishing word to the disciples. She reported a missing body and an incredible encounter with two angelic messengers from God. The messengers told her Jesus was alive, raised from the dead.

Peter and John hurried to the tomb and inspected the empty sepulcher. Puzzled, they waited and wondered. Within days, Jesus made at least two appearances to them and the rest of the disciples. Now, Jesus came for a final visit and some concluding words.

Specifically, He addressed Peter. "Simon Peter, do you love me?"

"Of course I love you."

Jesus said, "Then feed my sheep."

Jesus asked a second time. "Simon, do you love me?" Peter answered as before. Jesus gave him the command again, "Feed my sheep."

A third time Jesus interrogated Peter, "Do you love me?"

Tearfully, Peter declared, "Lord, you know everything, you know I love you."

"Simon, feed my sheep" (John 21:15-17).

Dramatically, Jesus asked Peter the question three times. I believe he asked it three times because Peter had denied him three times. Every time He asked the question, "Do you love me?" the question of the maiden in the courtyard reverberated in Peter's mind. "Are you one of his?"

Jesus forced Peter to relive every painful denial. By asking him to relive it, he gave Peter the opportunity of forgiveness for it.

Jesus taught us a lesson here. He didn't reject Peter just because Peter had rejected Him. Jesus wanted him to know God responded differently from what he expected. God still valued him. God had work for him to do. Sin didn't disqualify him for service and guilt didn't cut him off from a relationship with Jesus. Jesus offered Peter the opportunity of restoration.

We cannot see the physical response of these two men to each other. We can imagine it, though.

I can see Jesus put His arm around Peter's shoulder. Peter stood with eyes lowered, not daring to look into Jesus' face. Jesus patted Peter on the back and spoke gently, "Simon, do you love me?" With those words, Jesus gave

Peter an opportunity to reaffirm the love relationship he genuinely had for him.

By asking Peter these questions, Jesus said to him, "Peter, I know you failed me, but I also know you love me. I want you to express your love again. I want you to know my love for you remains intact. Though your denial makes you feel like you broke it, our relationship remains strong."

So often our transgressions cause broken relationships with other people and with the God we worship. We make a promise to someone, then break it. The broken promise also breaches the friendship. We find it difficult to overcome the distance between us. We transgress a standard of the God we worship. We find it impossible to step over the gulf to God again. Thankfully, however, the God of our faith has stepped over the gulf toward us. He has extended Himself to breach the separation.

The message of faith makes this plain. God stepped into our world to heal and restore a broken friendship. I like the way the apostle Paul said it. "You were dead in your trespasses and sins, in which you used to live .... But because of His great love for us, God, who is rich in mercy, made us alive with Christ."

"Alive with Christ!" In relationship with God! Freed from our transgressions! What a gift!

In his novel, *A Tale of Two Cities,* Charles Dickens introduced us to two men—Charles Darnay and Sydney Carton. Darnay, the innocent Frenchman, ended up a victim of the feverish evil of the French Revolution. The people have sentenced him to die at the guillotine. Carton, on the other hand, lived life without much thought to conscience. But, he and Darnay became friends. Knowing of Darnay's fate, Carton decided upon a scheme. He planned to exchange places with Darnay, to sacrifice himself for the life of another.

The night before the execution, Carton enters the prison for a final visit with his friend. He drugs him, changes clothes with him, and ushers him out. The inattentive guards notice nothing.

The next day, Carton faced the guillotine. A frightened young girl faced him, searching for bravery. She recognized he's not Darnay. Astonished, she asks, "Are you dying for him?"

"And for his wife and child."

He climbed the stairs to his death. He died

thinking, "It is a far, far better thing I do than I have ever done."

Dickens told us the story of a *guilty* man dying for an *innocent* friend. We marvel at the love so pictured. The scriptures tell us the story of an *innocent* man dying for *guilty* friends. God provided Jesus to give us a way of restoration with others and with our God. In the land beyond guilt, broken relationships find a place of reconciliation.

In the story of the Holy Grail, we hear the hope of the maiden who first told Sir Percivale of the Grail. Prayerfully, she said to him, "Perchance the vision may be seen by thee and those, and all the world be healed."

Healing from our guilt—we all pursue that Holy Cup, don't we? If we find it, we will discover a land filled with the blessings of self-acceptance, innocence, inner peace, love for others and restoration with God. That's a land worth discovering.

About the Author

GARY E. PARKER is a graduate of Furman, Southeastern Baptist Theological Seminary, and Baylor University. At Baylor he was a doctoral fellow with Dr. Dan McGee in Christian Ethics.

He has pastored churches in North and South Carolina as well as in Texas; at present he is pastor of First Baptist Church, Jefferson City, Missouri.

He is author of *A Shadow of a Doubt, The Gift of Doubt,* and *Principles Worth Protecting. The Guilt Trip* is his fifth book.